RARE STEAK, RED WINE, HOT TANGO!

A rollicking memoir of Argentina

HELEN WILKIE

\

All the sketches in this book were created by the author.

Rare Steak, Red Wine, Hot Tango!
©2017 Helen Wilkie
ISBN 978-0968462690

PRAISE FOR "RARE STEAK, RED WINE, HOT TANGO!"

"We have had the unique honour of being Helen's friends, part-time readers and travelling companions. We've been lost together, wandered the streets of her favourite neighbourhoods in her second home and savoured many a fine steak with the very best Malbec Argentina has to offer. In her newest book she regales us with story after story of her adventures — she elegantly takes us back to the times we shared with her in this extraordinary country." — *Susan and Michael, Fellow Travellers*

"Can a city really be magical? That's the feeling you get when you read *Rare Steak, Red Wine, Hot Tango*! Helen Wilkie paints a picture of the vivacious people, spectacular landscape and quirky culture that captured her heart. I've never been to Buenos Aires, Argentina, but this book has awakened my interest. It's beautifully written, with each chapter focusing on one amusing anecdote, including some sketches by the author herself. It could be a travel guide for anyone who wants to visit, but you don't even need to book an airline ticket. Just sit back (perhaps with a glass of red wine), read the book, and imagine you're already there. Then, if the feeling takes hold of you, book your ticket and prepare to kick up your heels with hot tango. This book takes you to Buenos Aires, whichever path you choose." — *Lynda Goldman*

"Expressively written, Helen's book paints word pictures akin to her watercolours. I am there with her during her adventures, feeling the atmosphere, seeing the scene, hearing the music. Argentina owes her a debt!" — *Sharon Chandler*

To Susan Birkenshaw and Lois Ferguson, my Butt Kickers. It's thanks to their encouragement and support that I have now finished this, my 9th and favourite book, as well as all the others.

To all my friends in Buenos Aires, those who are mentioned in the book and those who are simply part of the reason I love Argentina so much.

Gracias a todos!

CONTENTS

INTRODUCTION

In January 2014, at an age when I thought such notions well behind me, I fell in love. Deeply, madly and forever.

Not with a person, but with a place.

The object of my affection, my desire, my love is the beautiful, quirky, maddening, magical city of Buenos Aires, Argentina.

The love affair grew over several visits, each longer than the last, each one deepening my passion. Now, I spend several months of every year in Buenos Aires.

Now Buenos Aires is mine for life!

How is it possible to fall in love with a place? Especially a big, bustling, busy city?

I don't know. I only know I did from the moment I set foot on Argentine soil.

Buenos Aires has been on my bucket list for so long I don't even know how it started. I think it might be something to do with the name itself. *Buenos Aires*. It's a delicious name, isn't it? It means "good air", which is apparently how it struck Spanish explorer Pedro de Mendoza when he landed here in 1536. Like any other big city, its air is nothing special now, but it's not about the meaning — it's about the sound of the words.

Have you ever noticed how a lover's name feels on your tongue? That warm, soft sensation? That's how I feel about the name *Buenos Aires*, because that's what I feel for this city: love.

Attending a conference a few months before my first visit, I met a couple of women who had both recently been in Argentina, and the more they talked the more I wanted to see it for myself. I finally asked myself why I didn't just go, and came up with no good reason. So in January 2014 I simply booked a flight and a hotel and came.

Although I came by myself, I wasn't completely without resources. My speaker colleague Jeanne Martinson had been here on a trip, and she put me in touch with Cecilia, a local guide. She was lovely. On that first trip I was her client, but we have since become fast friends, and she features in a number of the stories in this book — or, as Cecilia calls them, *aventuras*!

Eleanore is a friend of my youth in Scotland, whom I see when I visit my family there. She expressed an interest in coming to Argentina in November 2014 if I would come back and meet her here. At first that seemed a bit over-ambitious, but after being here two days, I emailed her, "I'm in! Let's do it!" So I had two two-week vacations here in one year!

But even then I knew vacations wouldn't be enough. I didn't want to be a tourist here — I wanted more. I was smitten, and I couldn't get enough of Buenos Aires.

For months after that second visit, back in Canada — where I have lots of friends and a very good life — all I could think of was how soon I could come back and how long I could stay.

As a writer, I am fortunate in the work that I do. I have clients in several countries — professionals whose books I help write or even ghostwrite — so I can work anywhere. So why not beautiful Buenos Aires? My plans came together in late 2015.

My friends Susan and Michael had been spending six months of every year in Cuenca, Ecuador for years, so I decided to spend Christmas and New Year with them and then fly to Buenos Aires in early January 2016.

I would be here for three months. No tourist I this time — now I was an Honorary Porteña! (Natives of Buenos Aires are called Porteños, because they are people of the port city. Although I wasn't born here, I happily claim honorary status.)

During A3 (as Susan called my third Argentine adventure), I travelled and saw some other parts of this fascinating country and met many of its people — these trips feature in some of the stories in the book.

My Swiss friend Claudia, whom I met during A3, emailed me the day before leaving to go home to Zurich. She said she felt like a carrot being pulled out of the ground, she so wanted to stay. Obviously, the Buenos Aires mystique pulls on many others besides me.

As a matter of fact, quite a few of my expat friends came here on vacation and loved it so much they just stayed on. The day before I left to come back to Toronto at the end of A3, my friend Venetia took me out to breakfast. She asked me why I was going home. I said it was because my three months were up, to which she replied, "I know, but you don't want to go. Why don't you just stay?"

Oh my, how tempting was that?

But I knew I couldn't just stay. I had to go back to Toronto and consider this carefully, far from the seductive influence of tango and silky smooth Malbec — far from Buenos Aires.

I did seriously consider it. "Why not?" I asked myself. Why not just pack up and move to Argentina? After all, I'd done that once before, when I moved from my native Scotland to Canada.

In the end, though, I chose a different route. I'm happily and proudly Canadian, and I love Canada. I didn't want to give it up. So I decided to follow Susan and Michael's pattern — half the year in Canada and almost half in Argentina and its neighbouring countries.

As I write this, it's my first half-year term (A4). I've exchanged Canadian winter for Argentine summer. As long as I'm fit and healthy, I plan to do this for many years to come — as my old

American boss used to say, "The good Lord willin' and the creek don't rise."

The stories in this book come from the various trips, hopefully supplemented by those that will happen during A4 and future "A"s. I hope they'll give you a taste of *mi Buenos Aires Querido* as tango legend Carlos Gardel called it — my beloved Buenos Aires — and maybe you'll decide to visit. Be warned though — it gets under your skin and into your heart.

Chapter One

TAXI!

It was my first visit to Buenos Aires. I'd been here for a couple of weeks, and my holiday was winding down. My plan for this particular day was to go to the *Microcentro* (downtown) and have a last lazy wander around shops and cafes.

As usual on that trip, I hopped in a taxi. My Spanish was improving but still tentative, and I always took any opportunity to practise. The driver was surprised and pleased at my efforts, and immediately engaged me in conversation. He introduced himself as Julio and asked me the usual first question, "Where are you from?" So we were on first-name terms right away, and within minutes I knew all about Julio. A short, round man with white hair, he looked a bit like Santa Claus. He was in his sixties, a widower with grown children who lived in another city.

He asked me my purpose in going to the *Micro*, and I made the mistake of mentioning shopping. He immediately asked if I was interested in leather.

Argentina is justly famous for its leather — a byproduct of all that beef — and leather jackets are usually high on any tourist's list. I had, in fact, already bought a great leather vest that delighted me and wasn't in the market for more. But that didn't faze Julio.

Calle Murillo is a street with one leather store after another, and that's where I had bought my vest. When I told Julio this, however, he made the Spanish equivalent of "pshaw!" With a disgusted look, he told me that wasn't the place to go. "They don't have any style there — just leather." With that I realized why I hadn't liked many of the jackets I'd tried there — he was right, they had none of the style I'd seen in the more fashionable (and expensive) downtown stores.

Naturally, Julio had a much better alternative! I told him I didn't want any more leather, but he didn't give up easily. I knew that, like taxi drivers in many major cities with a big dependency on tourists, Julio would have a commission arrangement with certain establishments. Everybody has to make a living, so I have no quarrel with that as long as there's no coercion.

Julio knew of a leather factory a little outside the downtown area that he was certain a "fashionable lady like you" would love. He offered to take me there and bring me back downtown for a very reasonable flat fee.

Now when I told my friends back home this story, they were horrified. A strange driver, a strange factory in a strange area — what was I thinking? Well, I did think about it for a minute, but when you're travelling sometimes you just have to go with your gut. So I told Julio "*Dale!*" (let's go) and off we went. (As a precaution, I made sure he saw that I was following our route on the map.)

We had driven for maybe fifteen minutes, through areas I can only describe as "industrial", when we finally pulled up in a narrow street. I saw no sign of any shops, but the street was lined with taxis, which I took as a good sign.

There was no storefront, just a rollup door like a garage.

Suddenly it opened, and a young family emerged, complete with two laughing kids and many shopping bags. Another good sign. I followed Julio inside. He said he would have a coffee at the back while I shopped, and after reassuring myself he was not going to abandon me there, I moved towards the racks of multi-coloured leather jackets and shelves of lovely, stylish leather bags. I already had my vest though, and I was definitely not going to buy anything.

It was the colour that did it. Out of the corner of my eye, something in a soft muted orange tone beckoned. It turned out to be a shirt made of the finest, softest kid I'd ever seen. If I ever saw something like this back in Toronto, the price would have been three times what it was here. They only had one and it was my size. Game over!

I knew I didn't have enough cash, so I happily handed over my debit card. A moment later, to my chagrin, it was declined! It took me only a moment to realize what had happened, so let me back up a little to explain.

To get pesos in Argentina, I use my debit card at the bank machines to withdraw directly from my bank account in Canada. This works, but the daily limit is quite low, and I had already withdrawn cash that morning. The shirt would have put it over the limit, so it didn't work.

I know what you're thinking — credit card, right? But so many people had given me dire warnings about street theft (which I have never actually seen) that I never carried it except when travelling. I could see my lovely kid shirt fading into a dream.

But wait — here came Julio, asking what was wrong. I explained. He asked how much the shirt cost. I told him.

"I can lend it to you," he said, to my amazement. Of course I said no, but he offered again. "I have money in my car. Wait here and I will get it." (I guess Julio could see his commission fading away with the shirt.) I explained the daily limit problem and said I wouldn't be able to get the money for him that day.

"No problem, Señora," he said. "You can give it to me tomorrow."

I couldn't believe my ears. Bear in mind, this man didn't know me from Adam, and as he had picked me up at the taxi stand he didn't even know where I was staying!

Anyway, off he went to his car. When he returned, he peeled exactly the right amount from a thick wad of pesos, and I happily took possession of my beautiful shirt.

We arranged to meet next day at the taxi stand, where I repaid him as promised.

OK, maybe I took a chance when I followed my gut and let Julio take me to the leather factory. But he certainly took a chance by lending a substantial sum of money to me, a total stranger in his country. I think there's a lesson in human relations there.

Anyway, I smile and think of Julio every time I put on my lovely kid shirt!

Chapter Two

DIVA!

My friend Eleanore was visiting from Scotland, and Cecilia had accompanied us on a downtown shopping expedition. I use the word "expedition" advisedly, because when it comes to shopping, Eleanore is in a class by herself. She is intrepid, and never seems to tire.

On this particular day, we had been at it for several hours, on one of Buenos Aires' hottest, muggiest summer days, and we had reached the stage of ducking into the stores just for the air conditioning. After receiving a call on her cellphone, Cecilia announced that we were invited to a concert at the Catholic University of Argentina. It would feature an orchestra and two famous opera singers. That sounded lovely, and Eleanore and I were planning to go home for a refreshing shower and shampoo to get ready.

"No no!" said Cecilia, "we must go now. We will meet my friend Luis at his office and then we will go to the concert together."

So instead of appearing all cleaned up and freshly dressed, we dragged ourselves, hot and tired and laden down with shopping bags, to the headquarters of La Prefectura Naval Argentina (the Naval Police), where Luis worked.

Argentine men of a certain age have a lovely old world attitude towards women, and Luis couldn't have been more charming as he entertained us to coffee in his office. He spoke no English, and as Eleanore doesn't speak Spanish it was a mix of two conversations, interrupted by translation both ways and lots of laughter.

After our coffee and chat, a limousine arrived to carry us — shopping bags and all — to the university. Suddenly I didn't feel weary at all as I looked forward to this new experience.

The early arrivals were sifting into the auditorium as we walked up the broad steps of this modern building, which was in stark contrast to the lovely classical buildings of the University of Buenos Aires. Although I couldn't put my finger on the exact reason, there was a definite military feel to the whole thing that was quite intriguing.

Catholic University of Argentina

The orchestra and two singers were rehearsing, and it certainly sounded promising. Luis took us up to the front and introduced us to several notable guests, as well as the singers — who duly kissed us on both cheeks in the charming Argentine manner I had quickly become accustomed to.

Eleanore commented to me that the whole thing felt kind of surreal, and it did. To be fair, finding yourself in your street clothes surrounded by beautiful people in their finery will do that!

Finally, orchestra and singers disappeared to dress for the performance, and when they returned the military ambiance was explained. It was the orchestra of the Prefectura in full dress uniform!

They launched into an excellent two-hour performance that held us spellbound. And the singing! Oh my, the singing!

The man was an Italian tenor called Gianni Summa, and the woman was an operatic soprano called Diana Maria. You can see a 10-minute excerpt from this very concert on YouTube at https://www.youtube.com/watch?v=JESraGnRVoE .

(The singing starts at about the 5:20 mark.) When Gianni inviting "todos" to join in, you can bet we were singing along with everyone else. In fact, when I watched the standing ovation at the end, I was tickled to see Eleanore and me for a second or two as the camera panned by — if you know me, see if you can spot us!

Some days later I was having lunch with an Argentine business acquaintance, and he expressed envy that we had met the great Diana María, famous throughout Latin America. And she had welcomed us with a kiss!

It just goes to show that when an adventure offers itself you should take it — even if you are in your grubby clothes after a shopping trip!

Chapter Three

CARNIVAL!

When someone mentions carnival, you automatically think of Rio, don't you? And it's true that Rio has the biggest and most well known carnival in the world.

But the second largest carnival in South America is in Argentina, in a place called Gualeguaychu (pronounced Gwaleg-weyechoo). People from all over South America and beyond flock there every year, and for one week in February the population of this midsize city explodes as Gualeguaychu turns into Party Central. I was determined not to miss this.

It's a three-hour drive north of Buenos Aires, so Cecilia, her friend Donna from California, Cecilia's daughter Macarena and her friend Daniela all piled into Cecilia's heroic little car early in the morning and we hit the road for one of the best *aventuras* ever.

Our air-conditioning was tested to the limit on the journey, and when we arrived at our cabaña outside Gualeguaychu we all collapsed on the beds for a wee rest, followed quickly by a long-awaited dip in the pool. Ah well, even lukewarm water is wet!

Our show tickets were for the next night, so after a quick dinner we set out to explore the city.

Outside the *Corsodromo*, where the show would take place,

colourful stalls lined the streets, with vendors selling all the carnival paraphernalia. I couldn't resist buying a mask, even though I suspected it wouldn't survive the trip back to Canada.

*My carnival mask —
unfortunately it didn't
survive the trip back to
Canada!*

But most of the action this night was in the river. No, that's not a typo — I do mean IN the river. Along the *costanera* (river bank) were throngs of young people getting an early start on the party. Apparently they almost all quickly gave in to the lure of the water — I'm not sure how you can dance salsa waist high in the river, but somehow they were managing it.

We contented ourselves with watching, then stocked up on Malbec and headed back to the cabaña, where we lounged under the stars till the wee hours.

We all woke up next day full of excitement — until we saw the weather. Oh boy. Drizzling. Overcast. Emphatically not the weather we wanted for carnival.

But it was early — surely it would clear up in time. Although not sunny, it was already hot, so a dip in the pool buoyed our spirits and we set out to explore the town. We all wore our carnival finery, determined to have a great time.

A couple of hours before show time, we headed to a pizza place with a nice patio. The rain held off.

Until we sat down to eat.

Then the heavens opened. I've never seen rain turn so heavy, so quickly. The sky that had been pale grey now turned so black it looked like midnight, even though it was only seven o'clock.

Suddenly the sky was bright again — with sheet lightning! Oh yes, we had it all that night.

We were just across from the *corsodromo*, so a quick dash took us into the grounds, and under the nearest roof. Of course everyone else had the same idea, so hundreds of us were crammed into any space with a cover.

Actually, calling it cover was a joke. This slanting rain penetrated everything, and the sandy paths quickly turned into mud. I was starting to imagine headlines of disaster in next morning's newspaper.

We gamely put up with this for over an hour before deciding it wasn't going to stop and we should give up and go back to our cabaña.

But even that wasn't easy. Macarena and Daniela, who had elected to go and have their own adventures while we were at the show, were supposed to meet us at the car, but none of us had expected it to be this early. So, not knowing if they would even be there (cellphone reception having somehow melted away in the rain), we headed in the direction of the parking lot.

By this time the rain wasn't just coming down, it was what we in Scotland call "raining up the way" — bouncing off the cobblestones, creating rivers of fast flowing water that reached literally up to our ankles. I don't know if you've trudged over wet cobblestones, but they're slippery, which slowed us down even more.

Eventually, after what felt like days, we found the car. Thankfully, the girls were there waiting for us, and we all piled in.

Rain gear hadn't helped, and we arrived home like drowned rats. Despite the soaking, we weren't really unhappy about it all. Maybe a little disappointed at missing the big show, but as we women often do, we managed to laugh at ourselves as we peeled off our party clothes and poured generous glasses of Malbec.

———

Next morning dawned grey and overcast, and we considered going home early. Fortunately, Macarena and Daniela talked us out of that!

Back into town we went. Cecilia marched up to the *Corsodromo* box office and demanded rain check tickets for that night — and got them.

The weather unfolded the opposite way from the day before, dull all day and then the sun — a very hot sun — broke through in late afternoon.

The show started at 10 pm and lasted till about 3 am — everything happens late in Argentina!

So Cecilia, Donna and I arrived about 9.45 pm and headed for our seats in the second row. The lady who showed us to our seats did so with a stern warning:

"You will see many lovely boys tonight, but you must not touch them."

I'm not sure why she felt compelled to tell us this, although it gave us a chuckle. But when the show started we could see what she meant! Lovely boys and girls galore — and most of them almost naked! I've never seen so many beautiful people in one place.

The music started and nobody, including us, could stay in the seats. We clapped and danced all night as huge, amazingly intricate floats slowly moved past, many with a few of those beautiful people dancing on them or hanging tantalizingly from trapeze bars that swung out over the crowd.

One of the lovely boys we were warned not to touch!

The costumes got blingier and skimpier as the parade went on, and the dancers were more than happy to come to the side and pose for photos. We couldn't get in on this because we were in the second row, so we didn't touch the lovely boys — but only because we couldn't reach them!

There was one float that represented motherhood, with a lot of appropriate symbolism. The dancers who followed were led by a stunning young woman in a couple of strips of bling, body tanned and oiled — and several months pregnant! Proudly displaying her swollen belly, she danced as vigorously as the others in her sky-high-heeled boots. She was wonderful!

So we were very happy when we arrived back at the cabaña afterwards. It was after 3 am, but we still took time for a glass of Campari under the stars before falling into bed. There's something magical about relaxing outdoors in the middle of the night. We were actually tempted to sleep out there, but decided that several hours in deck chairs might cramp our style for next day.

Carnival was done — but our adventure wasn't quite over yet!

———

The sun was bright and hot when we left after breakfast next morning. Despite the heat, the heavy rain of the past two days had sunk deep into the dirt roads around Gualeguaychu, and the traffic had churned them into a quagmire. Cecilia had to drive very slowly, looking for rocks and the odd dry spot to get us through.

Half an hour out of town, in the midst of fields on all sides, our luck ran out.

We drove into a rut, squelched into the mud and came to a halt, wheels spinning helplessly beneath us.

"No problem," said Macarena brightly, "We'll get out of this in a few minutes." Have you ever heard the expression, "If you want to make the gods laugh, tell them your plans"? Well, the chatter of the parakeets high above our heads sounded to me exactly like celestial laughter!

The girls pushed fallen branches under the front wheels, only to see them sink at the first move. They tried rocks next — they sank too. How deep *was* this mud?

By this time the sun was high in the sky, and the few trees in the area were too tall to offer any shade. So we all slowly broiled as the girls tried everything to get the car out, without success.

This narrow road was the only way out of Gualeguaychu, but

apparently we were the only ones leaving, as we saw hardly any traffic.

One fellow on a motor bike told us there was a main road a mile or so further on, and a place where we might hire someone with a tractor to pull us out. After an hour or so of grim, futile effort, Cecilia, Donna and I decided to go for it.

Off we trudged, the heat becoming more oppressive by the minute. Cecilia, ever the optimist, reminded us that this was an *aventura*. That it was!

Ten minutes on, I happened to turn around and noticed some action back around the car. Besides Macarena and Daniela there were a couple more people and — a horse!

We found out later that a young boy had seen our predicament, gone home and fetched his father with the horse. Said horse was hitched to the car and had it out in no time. A minute later the girls drove up beaming and picked us up.

I've always wished we had stayed with the car so that I could have made a movie of our rescue by this equine hero!

So, was that the end of our *aventura*? Well no, not quite yet.

———

All five of us were liberally spattered with dark, rapidly drying mud. Stinky mud. The prospect of a four-hour drive to Buenos Aires in the confines of the car wasn't a pleasant one.

Suddenly Cecilia remembered there was a thermal spa in the area — which we had thought of visiting but decided we didn't have time. Well, now we would definitely make time!

Taking a slight diversion, we were soon driving through the luxurious gates of *Termas del Guaychu*, clearly a high-end spa. People sprawled in several outdoor pools full of blue, blue water — as well as one full of greenish water with steam rising off the surface: the thermal pool.

I can only imagine what the other guests thought when five laughing, mud-covered women invaded their oasis.

Digging through the trunk for our swimsuits, we were soon headed for the showers. That was a relief in itself, but when we lowered ourselves into those warm, caressing thermal waters — a-a-ah! I've rarely known such bliss!

And so ended the never-to-be-forgotten Gualeguaychu carnival adventure.

If you decide to go there — and I do recommend it — take rain gear as well as cool clothes.

And if you get stuck in the mud — wait for the horse!

Chapter Four

59!

A1 and A2 were just short vacations, so I took taxis everywhere. But of course, you don't get to know a city looking out the window of a taxi, so starting in A3, I changed all that. I vowed to learn and use the public transportation system, which includes a network of buses, subways and local trains.

THE TRAIN

To get to Cecilia's house in Olivos, which is in Buenos Aires Province, I took the train from the central hub of Retiro. The trains are fast, clean and modern, and the trip takes about 20 minutes. But the best thing is the on-board entertainment.

Sadly, there are poor people who jump on the trains and beg for money. Argentines generally are caring people, and usually these folks can count on gathering a few pesos.

But the entertainers are different. The first I saw was a young guy playing a violin — the distinctive sound of tango music reached my ears before I saw him. With each song — from tango to Broadway show tunes and lots in between — he drew loud applause, and when he came through the coach after several stations, the crowd showed its appreciation with generous donations.

Another day it was the ubiquitous Colombians with their mountain music. There were three of them, and they brought a complete sound system with them! As they arrived in each coach they set up their microphones in moments and were ready to start playing as the train moved off. They too were rewarded for their show.

But my favourite wasn't entertainment in the usual sense, although it certainly was a show.

The young man, maybe in his thirties, stood in the passage and set down a big cardboard box on the floor in front of him. As the train moved off, he addressed the travellers in a strong, clear voice. My Spanish was challenged because he spoke quickly, but it went something like this:

"Good morning ladies and gentlemen. Forgive me for interrupting your journey, but today I have a great opportunity for you."

With that, he opened his box and brought out a colourful bundle.

"I have for you the opportunity to obtain these top quality socks at an incredibly low price."

He then proceeded to demonstrate their colour, expandability and value.

"And these are available to you today for the very attractive price of only 40 pesos for 3 pairs."

After quite a bit more in this vein, he came around and sold his socks to those who were interested — and there were quite a few customers.

The socks actually were good value but I think the real reason he did so well was that, instead of the more common appeal for help, he proudly made a presentation, and the crowd responded.

As a professional speaker, I always appreciate a good presentation — and I have the socks to prove it!

THE SUBTE

The Subte, short for *Subterraneo*, is the Buenos Aires subway. I have no stories about the Subte because I've only been on it twice and didn't like it much.

There are currently six Subte lines, named A, B etc. The map designates them by colour code, but nobody seems to call them the blue line, the red line etc., preferring to use the letters. It's important to know which line you want, because they have different stations as well as routes.

The reason I've pretty much avoided the Subte is that, at least for now, none of the lines come into Recoleta, the barrio where I live. I did use it twice, when I was going somewhere best reached by Subte, and I found it to be hot, crowded and uncomfortable. Others' experience may be different, of course, but this is my memoir, so you get my opinion!

THE BUS

But the buses — now there's another story. The buses, known as *colectivos*, are where the fun is! (Just ask my friends Susan and Michael — but more on that in a moment.)

The great thing is that you can get anywhere in Buenos Aires, from the centre to the farthest suburban barrios, by bus. The not-so-great thing is that the system has about 3 gazillion buses, all flying around in wild abandon — and I use the word "system" loosely. There *is* a system, but I think you have to be a real *Porteño* (not an honorary one like me) to understand it.

Where to start? Well, let's begin with the bus stops. The most efficient are a group of stops known as the *Metrobus*, long stretches of pavement in the middle of major avenues, such as 9 de Julio, Cabildo and parts of Santa Fe. Each platform stop handles several different bus routes, and there are seats for you to wait. You simply find the sign for the bus you want, make sure you are on the right side and wait till it arrives. Very simple.

The other stops, though, are an adventure! Some of these do look like actual bus stops, but others are just poles inserted in the sidewalk, with two or three numbers painted on the side. Those numbers are the buses that stop there.

The ones that are obvious bus stops have poles too, but they have signs for each bus, giving a list of the stops from the beginning of the route to the end. It's wise to read these carefully, because you'll soon realize that even though, say, the 92, 93 and 130 all stop at your stop, their routes often bear no relationship to one another. So if you know the 92 is your bus and the 93 comes first, don't think that will do, because it probably won't. It may turn a corner you didn't expect and whisk you off in a totally different direction. I've been caught that way a few times!

Another false assumption made by visitors is that if the bus stop is designated for, say, the 152, that bus will automatically stop there. No, no, no. If none of the passengers wants to get off and nobody has clearly indicated they want to get on — the bus will fly past without even slowing down, leaving hapless tourists scratching their heads in confusion.

Let's say, for example, we're standing at a bus stop marked for the 59, 67 and 17. (This is just an example and I don't even know if such a stop exists, so please don't write in!) Along comes the 17, but the driver doesn't know if you want his bus (there are very few female bus drivers) or one of the others. His default is to fly blithely by.

Here's the trick. When you see your bus approaching, you stick your arm out, or preferably leap out onto the road just to make sure the driver sees you. *Then* he'll stop. Probably. Well, maybe.

The Buenos Aires buses don't "kneel" and the step is high. I've often said what might stop me coming down here is if my knees give out and I can't get on and off the buses!

The payment system is semi-automated. They don't take cash, so you have to buy a Sube (not to be confused with Subte), which is a plastic card that gets you on any vehicles in the system — train, Subte or bus. Before placing your Sube on a sensor, you first tell the driver where you're going and he hits a button that tells the system how much to charge. On the screen you can see how much you paid and how much is left on your card.

Now that's all fine if you're on the right bus!

Quite often, the bus that takes you where you want to go has the same number as the one that brings you back (although not always — that's too simple for Buenos Aires.) As all travellers know, it's quite easy to inadvertently stand on the wrong side of the road in a strange city, so although you may know you want the 110, you might easily catch the one going in the opposite direction.

Fortunately, when you tell the driver where you're going, he'll immediately spot the problem. He will tell you in rapid, colloquial Spanish, accompanied by hand signals, that you want the one on the other side of the street. Unfortunately, due to their habit of speeding off as soon as the doors close behind the last passenger, by the time you've figured this out you will be long past the stop.

At this point you will also discover that the distance between stops can be quite long, and rarely in a straight line. So you may find yourself deposited around two corners on a completely different street, with no clue how to get back on track. Isn't this fun?

Fortunately, *Porteños* are very friendly and willing to help. I try to always ask young people, because they will whip out their cell phones, go to Google Maps and figure it all out for you. Often they'll even walk you to where you're going.

You may be wondering why this chapter is called '59'. Well, therein lies a tale.

I had been dining out one evening with several friends at La Gran Parilla, a wonderful steakhouse in San Telmo, and we all spilled onto the street around midnight. Everyone went their separate ways, I with Venetia and Raul, who both live fairly near me. They knew an easy bus route home, so I followed along. Soon we emerged from San Telmo onto Avenida 9 de Julio, where a whole variety of buses stop at the Metrobus platforms along the avenue.

Raul declared we could take the 59, which would carry us along

Santa Fe and from there it would be an easy walk home, and that's
what we did.

The famous 59 Bus!

Fast forward to one day
during Susan and Michael's visit.
We had played tourist all day,
taking in Plaza de Mayo and all
its lovely surroundings, and then
enjoying *merienda* in Cafe
Tortoni. (*Merienda* is the
delightful custom of taking
pastries with coffee, or a glass of wine, around four in the afternoon, which nicely satisfies the stomach before the long wait until
the late Buenos Aires dinner time.)

Armed with my new bus knowledge, I led them to 9 de Julio
and the 59 bus. Unlike my earlier trip, when it was late at night and
quiet, this was rush hour — and extremely hot. In an effort to
make boarding faster, an official was outside with a Sube machine,
and everyone was processing their Subes at the stop. We stood in
line behind the commuters.

I duly told the official we were going to Callao and Guido and
he — I swear — said *Bueno*, and waved us through. The bus was
like the proverbial sardine can. I hadn't realized that Michael
doesn't like buses at the best of times, so this was not fun for him.

The jam-packed ride also made it difficult to see where we were
going, so it was some time before I realized I wasn't recognizing
any landmarks.

Eventually, most of the other riders left and we were able to sit
down. That's when Michael asked if I was sure we were going in
the right direction, and I had to admit I was pretty sure we
weren't! I was looking for streets I knew, but they just got less and
less familiar. I couldn't help also noticing that wherever we were, it
wasn't a very salubrious part of town.

Eventually, we had the bus to ourselves, and were soon turning
into what was clearly a bus terminal — we'd reached the end of
the line!

Fortunately, we all saw it as a bit of an *aventura* and happily went inside the terminal building to figure out what to do. Taking the straightforward route, I simply told the clerk we were lost. I told him where we wanted to go, and with a grin he said we could just take any of the buses. We soon found out that's because they were all 59 and all going on the same route — back the way we had come!

Before getting back to 9 de Julio, our bus wended its way through Constitucion and La Boca — neither of which were on our plans to visit, that day or any other.

I have a feeling that any time in the future when Susan and Michael and I reminisce about our travels, one episode that will always come up will be the tale of the 59 Bus!

Chapter Five

FUTBOL!

Like all of South America, Argentina is obsessed with soccer — or, as the world beyond North America calls it, football, converted phonetically into Spanish as *futbol*. Being originally from Scotland and having been married to a Portuguese man for many years, I'm also a fan of "the beautiful game".

In Buenos Aires there are several teams, but the great traditional rivalry is between Boca Juniors and River Plate. I had read that it was very dangerous for visitors to go to these games, and although it was possible to go with a tour group that didn't appeal to me, so I was resigned to missing the experience.

But one day in casual conversation, I discovered that Daniela was a Boca fan. Now of course anybody can claim to be a fan of any team without actually going to a match, but Daniela isn't that kind of fan. She actually goes to the game every week — by herself!

So I asked if I could go with her. She was surprised that I wanted to go, but delighted to take me.

There was, however, a small problem. Several years ago, to stop opposing fans from being shot (yes, shot), the rules were changed. So in order to get into the games, you have to be a "member". If not, you can't buy a ticket. Of course, Cecilia said that wasn't a problem and she'd figure it out. She went online, found a source and ordered a ticket for me. "Well, that was easy," I thought. Maybe a little too easy.

The day of the game, the seller came to deliver the ticket to Cecilia's house. Only it wasn't a ticket — it was someone's membership card. The member was a certain Mr. Zapata, and his photo was on the card. I would have to pass as Mr. Zapata to get in!

Nobody seemed concerned. They all told me just to slap the card on the machine at the turnstile and nobody would notice it wan't mine. With the stipulation that if I was stopped, Daniela would explain that I was Mr. Zapata's cousin, we set off. I could feel another Argentine *aventura* coming on!

———

Although I lived closer to the stadium, Daniela said we had to leave from Cecilia's house, because that's where the bus started and by the time it reached my place it would be full. So we duly left from Olivos, which is outside the city in Buenos Aires Province. Everyone on the bus was going to Boca, so obviously Daniela's strategy was the right one.

Daniela doesn't speak English, so my Spanish got a workout over the hour and a half it took to get there. There I was, speaking Spanish and going to the game on the bus — I really felt like a local that night!

Somehow I had expected the bus to go right to the stadium, but it didn't. We had to walk a few blocks — blocks seething with exuberant Boca fans. I was glad to be with someone who knew her way around.

Finally, we came to a narrow street at the end of which loomed the massive blue and yellow stadium. Because of its tiered, rounded shape, it's known as *La Bombonera* — the chocolate box. Daniela, however, referred to it in reverend tones as *El Templo* — the temple!

Our entry into *El Templo* was still some time away, as we were packed into the narrow street, shoulder-to-shoulder and moving slowly in concert with hundreds of other fans. Sounds like a nightmare, doesn't it? But it wasn't. Maybe that's because I was so caught up in the excitement of it all that I wasn't uncomfortable or afraid. I was having fun!

There was a police presence, but they seemed to be having just as good a time as everyone else — maybe only Boca fans are picked for that duty! People were shouting, laughing, singing — the decibel level was high, and so were the spirits.

Suddenly a voice came over the police loudspeaker: "Pregnant woman coming through!" Everyone dutifully moved to the left, and a very pregnant young woman with a toddler on her shoulder came through. No emergency — she was just a fan going to the game, and the usual South American reverence for pregnant women let her walk straight through to the turnstiles!

Ah yes, the turnstiles. I was starting to worry a bit about those. Daniela, who was behind me keeping a firm grip on my shoulders, yelled into my ear over the noise of the crowd. "Don't look at the guy in uniform. Just put the card on the reader and look straight ahead as you walk through."

I did as I was told, and went through with no problem — only to find there was a second turnstile before we got inside! I must have done OK, because minutes later we high-fived each other as we found ourselves inside the hallowed halls of *La Bombonera*. The electricity in the air was almost palpable.

While the tour groups made their way to the rarified air of the upper levels, I followed Daniela up the wide stairway, packed with *real* fans, to the General Admission section on the first level. Notice, I didn't say General Admission seats — because there were no seats. Just tiered concrete steps.

I can walk for many miles with no problem, but standing for long periods can be challenging. Now I was going to have to stand for at least the 45 minutes of the first half — no telling how much longer I could last.

Daniela, however, assured me if we moved fast we could get a seat for the 15-minute half-time intermission. When I asked her for more details, it turned out that when the half-time whistle blew, everyone sat down where they stood — and those who were too slow were left standing. More on that later!

I've been to many football matches throughout my life, but I've never felt an atmosphere like this one. Even before the game started, the thickening crowd was singing, punching the air, laughing. They were here to cheer on their heroes and they'd rather be in this place at this moment than anywhere else in the world.

La Bombonera is circular inside, with seats steeply tiered all around. Huge blue and yellow streamers looped high above the field, and young men took their lives in their hands to climb up on balconies and ledges to plant more Boca flags and banners!

The story of the colours is interesting — and somehow very Argentine. After they had decided to form a team called Boca Juniors, they realized they needed colours. The barrio of La Boca is built around the dock-

No safety net for this intrepid fan!

yards, so they decided to take the national colours of the next ship to dock. That ship turned out to be Swedish — so blue and yellow it was!

Suddenly the volume of the noise rose to eardrum-piercing level — the boys were coming onto the field! Like any sports team, it had crowd favourites. Here it was Carlos Tevez, known as Carlitos, a world star who had played for several top tier European teams and was now home to grace *La Bombonera* with his magic feet. I thought the noise was as loud as it could possibly get, but somehow it increased even more when Carlitos made his appearance.

The opposing team arrived to somewhat less of a welcome, and with the centre field formalities complete, the referee's whistle blew and the game began.

It wasn't the best football match I've ever seen, but the atmosphere more than made up for that. I couldn't join in the singing because I couldn't understand the words. (As she belted them out at the top of her voice, Daniela told me they were very rude!) But I punched the air rhythmically with the best of them.

Near the half-time mark, Daniela yelled in my ear that I should listen for the whistle — fat chance, in all this noise! I didn't hear it, but out of the corner of my eye I saw her disappear down below the heads. Before I could move, she grabbed my arm and pulled me down too. This was the promised half-time seat — on the steps we'd been standing on. And sure enough, dotted all around were people left standing because they weren't quick enough! Yes, there are definite advantages to coming with a local who knows the ropes.

The first half ended in a tie, and Daniela decided if we moved to another spot we would bring the team luck. I know, I know — but hey, I was having so much fun I was up for anything.

We spent the second half moving from one spot to another — none of which were as good as our first. But it looked as if Daniela's strategy was working, as Boca evened the score about a minute before the end. We were into extra time!

And it ended perfectly, when Carlitos scored the winning goal for Boca a few minutes in.

I can't even begin to describe the atmosphere then! Daniela and I jumped up and down, hugging each other and screaming till we almost fell over. Then we each jumped and screamed and hugged total strangers. (According to Daniela they weren't strangers — they were Boca fans!)

As we squeezed down the stairs with the crowd on our way out, I was amazed at the number of little children, toddlers, who were there. Sitting on parents' shoulders sporting their blue and yellow Boca hats, they weren't a bit fazed by the noise and frenzy. Get 'em while they're young!

By the time we reached the street it was about midnight, and I assumed we'd be headed for the bus. Wrong again!

"So," shouted Daniela, "shall we go for a beer?" Well I don't like beer much, but in for a penny ...

Then she asked if I liked chori. That's short for choripán, a kind of hot dog with a chorizo instead of a weiner. When I told her I'd never had one, Daniela decided that had to be fixed.

Crossing the street with the crowd, we found ourselves in a large parking lot, but instead of cars it was dotted with food stands. Each one was barbecuing chorizos for the chori, and the aroma was intoxicating. We duly slathered ours with who-knows-what from the condiment table (it was dark!) and went looking for beer. There seemed to be just a bunch of guys who had brought lots of beer and were selling it from coolers!

Beer and chori at midnight in the parking lot!

So there I was, standing in a parking lot at midnight, eating street food and drinking beer — bloody marvellous!

———

Now to find a taxi and head home. Well, that was the plan but it was easier said than done, as everyone else had the same idea. We decided to start walking and pick one up along the way. See previous comment.

I suddenly recognized where we were, and said to Daniela that I could catch the 130 bus here. She laughed, explaining that no buses stopped in the vicinity of *La Bombonera* for two hours after the game, because they didn't want buses full of rowdy fans! We kept walking.

Bear in mind that while my place was maybe 15 minutes away by bus, Daniela had to get all the way back to Olivos. I was starting to feel just a little uneasy. Daniela, on the other hand, seemed perfectly unconcerned.

As we flagged down taxi after taxi, all full, two men appeared alongside us — an older man and a younger one who might have been his son. The older one stated the obvious, that we were having trouble getting a taxi. Then he said their car was just around the corner and they could give us a ride.

My default response to that was a definite no, but to my surprise Daniela was telling them how far she had to go, and actually discussing their offer. It turned out they were from San Isidro, a town just on the other side of Olivos.

So now we were walking along the street after midnight with two strange men, on the way to their car — talking about the game! I pulled Daniela back and whispered, "Are you sure this is OK?"

"Oh sure," she replied, looking at me in surprise, "they are from San Isidro and they are Boca." Oh well then, I guess that made it OK!

So we turned a corner and climbed into the back of their car — I with some trepidation, I have to say. I was paying careful attention to the road to make sure they were taking us in the right direction, while Daniela was happily immersed in *futbol* talk.

The driver — the older man — caught my eye in the mirror and asked me where I was from. When I told him Canada, he asked if I was from the French or English part — I've noticed that most Argentines know at least this one fact about Canada. He then switched to perfect English and we chatted about my visit to Argentina. I was still a bit nervous, but I could see we were almost at my apartment. They dropped me off a few minutes later and headed for Olivos.

I've never been a hitchhiker, but even I know the #1 rule is that you never get in a car with more than one person, and here was Daniela driving off in the middle of the night with two strangers — even if they were Boca fans from San Isidro.

When I walked in my apartment door, my phone immediately pinged with a WhatsApp message from Cecilia, wanting to know if I had managed to get into the game as Mr. Zapata. I hesitantly told her we had a ride home with some people from San Isidro. "Excellent!" she replied, to my surprise. Nonetheless, I was very relieved to get her message soon afterwards saying Daniela had arrived home.

By going to see *futbol* at *La Bombonera*, I apparently achieved the dream of soccer fans around the world. It was certainly one of my all-time favourite *aventuras*.

Chapter Six

TANGO 1: TACONEANDO!

If you've never been to Buenos Aires, you may think — as I did before I came — that the tango is just a dance. But when you come here you soon realize it's so much more than that. Tango is part of the sound and the soul of Buenos Aires.

Tango has a long and spotty history. It was introduced by Italian and Spanish immigrants in the late 1800s. Poor dock-workers for the most part, they mostly came alone, hoping to make their fortunes, leaving wives and sweethearts back in Italy and Spain. It's said that the close embrace so symbolic of tango was an attempt to recreate the physical closeness they were missing.

The dance, and the music, grew and evolved among the poorer folks, notably in working class barrios like La Boca and San Telmo. In fact, it was many years before it became socially acceptable.

In the 1930s, a handsome young singer named Carlos Gardel became the first to actually sing tango music, as it had previously been an instrumental accompaniment to the dance. Gardel's songs, with their lyrics in the distinctive *lunfardo* slang of Buenos Aires, started a storm of controversy, but he became so popular he is now generally regarded as the Father of Tango.

Today, if you walk around the Caminito area of La Boca, or Plaza Dorrego in San Telmo, you can see people dancing tango in the streets. There is also a wide variety of tango shows, where you'll soon be mesmerized by the flying feet, serious expressions and sensuous movement of the dancers.

On my first visit to Buenos Aires, Cecilia took me to a small, intimate venue in San Telmo called Taconeando, to see my first tango show. I was instantly hooked! I loved the way the music and the dance moved fluidly from playful to melancholy and back. I loved the drama of the performance and the heart-tugging songs by male and female singers.

Most people I know admit that even if they speak Spanish they don't understand many of the song lyrics, but the music and the singing are enough to pull your heart out.

My sketch of the stage at El Viejo Almacen, another tango show venue, with bandoneonero

What makes tango music distinct from any other is the bandoneon, an instrument that is technically a type of concertina, but the melancholy sounds pulled out of it by tango musicians makes it unlike any other sound. In the hands of a master, the bandoneon weeps.

One fun aspect of the Taconeando show came at the end. The three pairs of dancers split up and invited audience members to dance. I was picked! Clearly I didn't know anything about tango, but my expert partner made it easy to glide around the cabaret floor as if I did.

The show ended, and the audience began to disperse. Cecilia and I were finishing a fine bottle of Malbec, and were eventually the only people left. I happened to notice a fellow leaning against a wall at the back, and recognized him as the male half of my favourite of the three couples. I mused aloud that it would be nice to have my photo taken with him. Cecilia leapt into action, asking if he would pose for a photo with her friend from Canada.

Now I thought I was going to stand beside this fellow for a quick photo, but he had other ideas. He was, after all, a performer. Taking my hand, he led me up onto the cabaret floor, under the lights. He took me into the traditional close embrace, pointed down and said, "The leg — up!" So I did as I was told, lifting my leg close to his — although I didn't quite have the nerve to wrap it around — and Cecilia snapped the moment on my iPhone.

I got more than I bargained for here!

This is the resulting photo, which drew a flurry of comments when I posted it next day on Facebook!

Thus began my ongoing love affair with tango.

Chapter Seven

TANGO 2: LESSONS!

When I came for my first longer-term stay in Buenos Aires, I was no longer content to watch tango — I wanted to dance!

Before I left, I had the good fortune to "meet" Linda Claire Puig online when I took her course, "Traveling with your Business Made Easy", which was very helpful to me in learning how to live and work here in Buenos Aires. (Great course, by the way. You can find information on the Resources page at the end of the book.)

She happened to mention she had been in Buenos Aires not too long before and had taken tango lessons from Alejandro Puerta, whom she highly recommended. I contacted him and set up my first lesson. Wow! Alejandro is a wonderful teacher, with an infectious love of tango, and I was hooked in the first ten minutes.

Unlike many teachers, he focuses not on set sequences, but on connection between the dancers and with the music. According to Alejandro, if you get that right, the rest will follow. I was, of course, a complete beginner, but it wasn't long before I felt I was actually dancing tango!

A word here about "Argentine tango". There is another form of "tango" you'll see in ballroom dancing, but it's quite different. In that form, the dancers hold each other far apart. In Argentine tango, they dance in close embrace, often cheek-to-cheek, with the embracing arm far around the partner. It's like dancing in a warm hug!

Unlike in the ballroom version, the upper bodies are in close contact, which maintains the connection, while the lower bodies stay further apart to allow room for fancy footwork.

I liken this comparison to whisky. In Scotland we know that ours is the only true whisky, so we don't call it Scotch – we just call it whisky. We know there are other drinks that call themselves "whiskey" — but who really cares? Nobody in Scotland!

In Buenos Aires, when we say tango we mean Argentine tango. Just as with whisky, we know there is another dance people call tango, but who really cares? Nobody in Argentina!

Towards the end of my first longer stay (A3), Cecilia and I went back to Taconeando — you'll remember that's the place where the dancers invite audience members to the stage after the show. I was chosen again, but this time it was different.

Tango lesson with Alejandro!

I can't speak for men learning to tango, but for the woman a lot depends on how well the partner leads. If you have a good leader, it's easy to follow. My partner that night was, of course, a professional *tanguero*, and I followed him like an old pro!

There were now only two couples in the show instead of three, which meant just four couples now shared the cabaret floor. The live tango orchestra was still playing, the audience still in their seats. I don't know how the others faired, but I felt as if I was in a world of my own.

Cecilia later asked me if I was self-conscious in front of the audience, and I could honestly say I forgot they were there.

But dancing with a teacher who leads like a dream is one thing; joining the throng at the *milonga* is something quite different.

Chapter Eight

TANGO 3: MILONGA!

As I said earlier, seeing tango danced at the shows intrigued me enough to take lessons and learn to dance myself. Private lessons were wonderful, and with Alejandro's help and encouragement I was soon making good progress.

One day, he said the fateful words, "OK Helen, you are ready for the *milonga*." Gulp! I was excited and terrified in equal measure.

Milongas are public dance halls where people go to dance tango. (Confusingly, *milonga* is also a style of tango, but here we're talking about the venues.) *Milongas* have sprung up in cities around the world, as the popularity of tango continues to grow. But the *milongas* of Buenos Aires, the home of the tango, are a world apart.

I've met people from several other countries who have come to Buenos Aires specifically to indulge their love of tango — and some never left!

Personally, I've always been intimidated by the whole idea. Why? Because I've heard so many stories about women never being asked to dance, or being embarrassed by an insensitive partner who felt they weren't good enough. The way I'd heard it, people who go to *milongas* are tango fanatics, and they won't dance with you unless they know you can dance. This, of course, is a

Catch-22, because how will they know you can dance if nobody dances with you?

But eventually, I began to feel stupid because, despite my professed love of tango, I hadn't ventured out to a *milonga*. Towards the end of A4, I resolved to put myself out there and give it a try.

At InterNations, one of the expat organizations I belong to, I had met an American woman called Lola, who was known as Tango Gypsy, and going by that handle she sounded like someone who could introduce me to the tango scene. Besides, I liked her, so I asked her to take me under her wing and she said she'd love to. (There is information about Lola's tango business on the Resources page.)

There are a host of *milongas* to choose from. You could dance tango every night of the week in a different place, and many people do. Having been dancing tango in Buenos Aires for fifteen years, Lola knows most of them. She explained that they all have their own styles, characteristics and even personalities. Some are quite snooty, while others are more welcoming to newbies. She decided we should start with Wednesday night at La Milonguita in Palermo. She also brought along Mary, a fellow American tango enthusiast who was visiting her in Buenos Aires.

So I dressed in the closest thing I had to tango clothes, packed my beautiful, authentic Argentine tango shoes, and mentally girded up my loins.

La Milonguita is in the hall of an Armenian church, but this is no "church basement" affair. Entering the venue is like stepping back about five decades. A lovely curved balcony allows spectators a fine view of the activity below, but most people were downstairs where the tango action was. And what action!

The evening starts at 7 pm with a class — as many do — but when we arrived at 8.30 pm the class was over and the *milonga* proper was well underway. Most *milongas* go on well into the wee hours, like all evening entertainment in Buenos Aires.

I can only describe the crowd here as eclectic: old ones, young ones, tall ones, short ones, fat ones, thin ones, *Porteños* and foreigners — all having a wonderful time expressing tango in their own ways. From the graceful *vals* to the lively *milonga* to the soulful *tango*, each variation of the dance has its own charm — although I haven't yet mastered the quick footwork of the *milonga*. That's my ambition for next year!

I feel like a different person in my tango shoes!

We sat down at one of the little tables around the floor that lent the place a cabaret air, and changed into our tango shoes — if you don't have the right shoes people will assume you are not serious. Actually, the tango shoes here are so beautiful that I couldn't wait to get a pair, and I love them.

My fears of wallflower status quickly proved unfounded as I received my first *cabeceo*, or invitation to dance. This is a very important protocol you must learn if you are going to the *milonga* in Buenos Aires.

When a man selects a woman to dance with, he doesn't just march right up and ask her, risking rejection and embarrassment. Instead, he tries to catch her eye, and when he does he makes a little questioning gesture with his head, and perhaps his eyebrows. To accept, the lady gives a little nod. If she doesn't want to dance with him, she simply won't catch his eye, so nobody is publicly embarrassed.

Anyway, I found myself the object of a *cabeceo* and duly gave the nod. My first partner of the evening was a *Porteño* who clearly knew his way around the *milonga*. His first move was to remove my glasses and place them on the table where I had been sitting! (I later saw other women take their glasses off to dance, so it's the norm, but I didn't know that then.)

He must have noticed my surprise, because as we moved onto the floor, he whispered seductively in my ear, "Señora, in tango you do not need to see — only feel." As silly as that may sound, it's actually true. Many people dance with their eyes closed — remember, it's about connection.

It soon became clear why he wanted my glasses off, because he immediately clutched me in a ferocious hug so tight that my glasses would have dug a furrow across his cheek! Dancing in this tight embrace was challenging as there wasn't much room for my feet, but I managed.

With each partner you dance a *tanda*, which consists of three or four tunes. Alejandro had explained that this gives you a chance to get used to each partner, and sometimes it may take one or two tunes for the connection to click in. I found that to be true.

I danced a few nice *tandas*, some with foreign visitors, reminding me that tango is Argentina's gift to the world (as well as Malbec of course!)

But the best *tanda* was a bit of a surprise. I received the *cabeceo* from an elderly man, short and balding with a little paunch — but very nattily dressed. When I accepted, he buttoned his jacket, came to my table and gave a little bow. When we arrived on the dance floor, he took me in his arms, but this was no overenthusiastic bear hug or tentative hold. This was the perfect tango embrace, close and intimate but not uncomfortably so. When we began to dance, he expertly led me into the turns, the *ochos* and other steps I had learned from Alejandro, and I followed him as easily as if we'd been dancing together for years. What a lovely experience! I haven't seen him since that night, but I keep hoping, as I would love to dance on a cloud with him again.

There's one more thing I want to say about the *milonga*. It occurred to me that we in North America worry too much about things that don't matter. On the dance floor I saw people of all ages, shapes and sizes, many wearing exotic tango clothes and bright jewellery. If this had been in Canada, we might have heard remarks like, *she doesn't have the legs for that skirt*, or *she should never have worn that dress with her figure*, or *she's way too old for that outfit*, or even *his hairpiece is really obvious*. Or we might snigger to see a man dancing with a woman almost a foot taller.

But here's the thing — THEY DON'T CARE! None of that matters to these tango lovers. They don't care what you look like, how old you are or what you're wearing. All that matters is tango. I watched them circle the floor with their eyes closed in ecstasy, as the soulful sound of tango music took over their being. Tango speaks to the soul, and everyone deserves this pleasure.

Tango gives these people an opportunity to make an intimate connection with someone who five minutes ago was a total stranger, and who in another five minutes would be a stranger again. But during the dance, they are connected in their core. Tango gives them an opportunity to express a sexuality that you'd never suspect if you met them anywhere outside the world of the *milonga*!

So there you have the story of my love affair with tango, so far. I now continue dancing when I'm in Toronto at some of the many schools and *milongas*, so each time I come back to Buenos Aires, my tango will be a little better.

If you come to Buenos Aires, you'll probably go to see a tango show and then perhaps take a lesson or two. If you do, from my heart I recommend Alejandro. You'll find information about how to contact him on the Resources page at the end of the book. Tell him I sent you!

Chapter Nine

WETLANDS!

In January 2016, Cecilia had a milestone birthday, and to celebrate she invited Donna and me to join her on a five-day trip to Los Esteros del Iberá, a massive wetlands region in Corrientes Province in the north of the country. This is not something I would have thought of myself, but I jumped at the chance to see a different face of Argentina. Besides, I've learned that any trip with Cecilia usually turns out to be an adventure, so why not?

It's an 800 kilometre drive, so we loaded up with provisions and set off early in the morning.

The plan was to drive to Mercedes, a small city in Entre Rios Province, where Cecilia has a friend (Cecilia has friends everywhere!) We would stay in Mercedes overnight and drive the rest of the way next day.

The drive was fairly uneventful until about 40 kilometres from Mercedes, when the state of the highway took a sudden turn for the worse. Potholes abounded, as well as wide areas of loose rubble. Several times we ended up in the path of oncoming traffic. It was quite alarming, and a great relief to arrive in Mercedes.

After settling into our little hotel, we set off to visit Cecilia's friend Claudia, who welcomed us with typical Argentine warmth

— and lots of Malbec. Cecilia and Claudia talked well into the wee hours, while Donna and I tried valiantly to improve our Spanish conversational skills.

———

Next morning we left right after breakfast as planned — and that was the last thing that went as planned.

We had been warned that the road from Mercedes to our destination was very bad. We dismissed that idea, thinking we had seen the worst of it the previous day. We were wrong. I think you'll get the picture when I tell you it was 115 kilometres — and it took us four hours!

The locals told us the government had suddenly stopped the funding for the road and that's why it was in such a state. Although Argentines play the "blame the government" game around everything, I'm quite prepared to believe it in this case, because it did look like a road under construction that had suddenly seen all work cease. If it had been in Canada, there would have been yellow tape around it to keep all traffic off.

Nonetheless, there being no other way to get there, we crawled and bumped along, our high spirits gradually sinking despite our best efforts. We stopped a couple of times for a break, but the searing heat quickly drove us back into our air-conditioned car.

A few kilometres outside the hamlet of Colonia Carlos Pellegrini, we began to notice some interesting wildlife that perked us up a bit. Huge, beautiful white birds erupted out of the marshes and soared high above us on massive wings, while a variety of smaller birds hopped around the edge of the road, watching us curiously.

Most exciting for me was the sight of capybaras grazing lazily by the roadside. Capybaras are the world's largest rodents, and they look like rats the size of pigs. I know they sound horrible, but it's one of those cases where they are so ugly they're cute! Locals call them *carpinchos*, and they are endemic throughout the region.

Finally — dusty, hot and tired — we arrived in Colonia Carlos Pellegrini and were escorted to our cabaña. And what a wonderful surprise that was! Inside a gated compound called Camba Cua, our quite luxurious cabin could have easily slept eight people, so we were able to spread ourselves out in air-conditioned comfort.

Carpincho by the roadside

It wasn't long before we discovered the pool — right outside our door. I think it was supposed to serve all the cabins — as was the outdoor *asado* — but in the four days we were there we had both exclusively to ourselves. And boy, did we make use of that pool!

I don't think I've ever been as hot as I was in Los Esteros del Iberá — and it was constant from morning till night. Fortunately we were never far away from Camba Cua, Carlos Pelegrini being a very small "colony", so we consoled ourselves with many dips in the pool each day, and sometimes again before bed.

Sometimes with Campari.

———

Our deal included a guide, a local man called Pedro, and our first guided venture was on the lake, Lago del Iberá. That experience delighted my very soul. We drifted silently over a plant-filled lake, full of birds and animals — including many *carpinchos* and even a moose. Funnily enough, as I had seen many moose at home in Canada and therefore didn't find it very exotic, that's the one that thrilled Cecilia.

But the most exciting sight was the crocodiles! OK, they were black caiman, which are a little smaller, but as far as I'm concerned a crocodile is a crocodile — especially when it's basking in the sun with its huge mouth open, displaying those lethal teeth!

Cecilia kept standing up in the boat to take photos, and I had visions of her falling overboard to become the object of a caiman feeding frenzy. Fortunately, that didn't happen and we made it safely back to the cabin for our *asado* — and therein lies another tale.

We had the use of a traditional outdoor *asado*, the Argentine version of a barbecue, which was a large brick structure with a sheltered seating area around it. We found the local butcher shop, which was actually in somebody's house, and bought the usual *asado* meat selection. The ever-friendly Cecilia had invited Pedro to join us, and he offered to cook. Bonus!

We lounged in the pool watching him do all the work, and then as it was too hot to eat outside we gathered around the big table in our cabin.

Our mouths were watering at the sight and smell of our feast — until we started eating it. After a few minutes of determined chewing with no noticeable result, I realized Pedro was the only one swallowing the meat! That was the first time I'd ever had meat so tough I couldn't swallow it.

Pedro said that had he known we were buying meat he would have directed us to someone who sold different meat for visitors. He explained that the reason for the tough meat lies in the land. Carlos Pellegrini has dirt roads surrounded by marsh and swamp for miles around. The cattle have no place to walk, so they just stand around the roadside and get no exercises — hence the tough meat. Pedro took most of the meat home for his family, whose teeth were more up to the challenge than ours.

Fortunately, we celebrated Cecilia's birthday in a local restaurant, enjoying the meat reserved for visitors! (More on that later.)

Pedro took us on two walks over the next couple of days. During the daytime walk, we were excited to catch a glimpse of energetic monkeys as they played and chattered high in the treetops. There's always something special about monkeys, isn't there? It's as if they liked playing this game of hide-and-seek with the humans far below, and their screeching had a definite air of laughter about it.

But the highlight was the night walk. Pedro drove us to the edge of heavily treed area near the lake, and handed us each a powerful flashlight. Warning us to be very quiet and stay close behind him, he stepped out onto a wooden boardwalk about a yard wide, and into the trees.

Almost immediately we saw a giant toad, the size of a small dog, sitting perfectly still on the path and showing no sign of moving for us. He watched, unblinking, smiling his wide toad smile as we gingerly stepped around him. I almost felt we should apologize for disturbing him, except that I don't think we had.

Pedro shone his light across the lake, and a dozen pairs of red eyes peered from the surface of the water, as the resting crocodiles lazily followed our progress. The boardwalk stretched way across the lagoon, and Pedro's practised eye helped us see a variety of animals we would never have noticed, hiding among the water plants.

The word *Iberá* is not Spanish. It's a corruption of the Guaraní words *y berá*, meaning "bright water", and that night Pedro showed us the reason for the name. Instructing us to switch off our flashlights, he pointed out onto the lake, and to our delight we saw a huge area of truly bright water, much larger and brighter than normal moonlight would have created. It was surreal, and very beautiful.

The most memorable moment, however, came on the way back, where the boardwalk left the water's edge and meandered back through the trees.

Pedro stopped suddenly, put his finger to his lips and whispered, "Don't worry — just come as quickly as you can." Looking down to the left, I saw the reason for this warning.

This guy came too close for comfort!

Jammed right up against the boardwalk, about 18" from our feet, lay a large black caiman, giant mouth wide open and hooded eyes alertly watching our progress! I've often heard people say, "My heart stopped," but I never really knew what it meant until that moment. He was so close! I'd only ever seen these sinister looking animals in the zoo or in movies. During the day, seeing them glide soundlessly across the water was thrilling — but this was something else again. The sudden cold knot in the pit of my stomach was a primal reaction to this too-close-for-comfort encounter with the wild.

Following Pedro's instructions, we stepped to the right edge of our narrow walkway. Our night visitor smiled his knowing crocodile smile as we slipped hurriedly past and on our way to our cabin — and a welcome glass of Malbec.

———

As I said earlier, we were there to celebrate Cecilia's birthday, which fell on the day after the adventure of the crocodile.

For such a small, out-of-the-way place, Colonia Carlos Pellegrini has a surprising number of restaurants. We found one we liked and reserved a table. Not a bit shy about her age, Cecilia told the *dueña* the reason for our dinner, and we looked forward to our little "party" that night.

I had brought a bottle of champagne from Buenos Aires, and I took it with me to the restaurant — I was pretty sure the owner wouldn't mind. Not only did she not mind, but when we arrived she presented us with another bottle as her birthday gift to

Cecilia, as well as one the cabaña owner had sent over — I guess it really does pay to advertise! So we had three bottles of champagne for three of us — and Donna doesn't drink!

We enjoyed a lovely dinner — of the meat they reserve for visitors, which was much better than our barbecue of the day before — and a bottle of Malbec.

Then it was time to open the bubbly. Besides us, the single room that was the restaurant had two other full tables. One held a young couple on their honeymoon, the other a young family with two little kids.

Cecilia called out to the room at large that it was her birthday, we had champagne and we'd love to have them join us — and they all did! I couldn't help thinking that if you did that in Canada, people would smile awkwardly and leave it at that. Here, it was accepted for the genuine invitation it was.

As the owner and the waiter were the only two not at the table, we invited them too. They accepted — and contributed yet another bottle of champagne!

What a party! The more champagne I drank, the more fluent my Spanish became — or at least that's how it sounded to me! It was a long way to go for a birthday party, but it was certainly one to remember.

———

Next morning in the pool, we made a decision that resulted in yet another act in our Esteros del Iberá adventure.

Remembering the unbelievably bad road into Colonia Carlos Pellegrini and not looking forward to that hellish four-hour drive, followed immediately by 9-1/2 hours to Buenos Aires, we came up with Plan B.

Cecilia's friends in Mercedes had said they would love to have given us a real Argentine *asado*, and that we should let them know when we would be back. Of course they probably weren't thinking we would be back three days later! However, in true Argentine style, they were delighted to welcome us.

That decided, we left Los Esteros del Iberá a day early, drove the horrendous road and then checked into the same Mercedes hotel for the night.

Claudia and Jorge's place was a *chacra*, a smaller version of an *estancia*, just on the edge of town. As we drove through its gates, the heady aroma of grilling meat was already wafting through the air.

First, we visited Jorge, already busy over the *asado*, which was built into a wall in the kitchen, and fired with hot coals. I've always thought this gave better flavour to meat than a gas fired barbecue, and this confirmed that belief.

As we stood in the big kitchen watching Jorge at work (I love watching other people cooking, don't you?), I glanced down at the floor and got a surprise. Sitting in the middle of the kitchen floor was a huge toad, just like the one we had seen on our walk with Pedro — wearing the same placid toad smile! When I pointed him out, Jorge casually answered, "Oh yes, he lives somewhere out back and he often takes a shortcut through the kitchen." I'm a city girl — stuff like this blows me away.

Taking a shortcut through the kitchen!

After a guided tour round the grounds and visit with Claudia's horses, we sat outside with our glasses of Malbec, and the *asado* experience began. The other-world atmosphere was complemented by the sounds of *chamamé*, the traditional folk music of the region, playing in the background.

The first item off the grill is usually sausages. Jorge had made his own, and they were so yummy we were in danger of using up our appetites before the main course arrived.

Next came chicken, followed by melt-in-the-mouth lamb.

But the main event was undoubtedly the beef — in this case beautifully cooked, succulent ribs. A silence descended over the table as we gave all our concentration to eating. Although I'd eaten great steaks in fine *parillas*, I think it was that night that I came to appreciate how special the authentic Argentine *asado* really is. *Gracias*, Jorge!

———

And so ended the great safari to the wetlands of the north, a glimpse of another Argentina I had never imagined.

Chapter Ten

NEW YEAR'S EVE!

I brought in New Year 2016 in Ecuador, while visiting Susan and Michael on my way to Argentina. By December 31, 2016, though, I was already six weeks into my next stint in Argentina, and wasn't sure how New Year's Eve would unfold.

Before I arrived, Cecilia had been checking out restaurants, but that was a non-starter. They were mainly interested in tourists, as was evident from the fact that you had to pay in US Dollars — and a lot of them. We needed an alternative.

I had read that fireworks were a major feature of New Year in Buenos Aires. Remember, New Year falls in high summer here, and I thought it might be nice to usher in 2017 under the stars and the fireworks. Cecilia took this on as a project and pulled off a truly spectacular event.

One of the best places to see fireworks is in Puerto Madero, a quite modern and very tony barrio down by the river. That's also where the aforesaid expensive restaurants were, but our plans didn't include them.

My friend Jo-Anne was visiting from Canada. Another new friend, Linda, whom I had previously met through our online businesses, was visiting from California. (She is the one who intro-

duced me to my tango teacher, Alejandro.) Linda was in Buenos
Aires for several weeks as part of an extended travel adventure.
And finally, Cecilia's sister Adriana was in from Rosario for New
Year. So we were a group of five adventurous women looking
forward to what would be a new experience for us all — especially
Jo-Anne and I who were used to chilly New Year's Eves in Canada!

We arrived about 8.30 pm to claim a good spot, and found one
on a paved area right on the water in sight of what's known as *La
Puente de la Mujer,* or Bridge of the Woman.

New Year's Eve fireworks over the beautiful Puente de la Mujer

(They tell me the design is supposed to represent the leg of a
woman tango dancer. Not sure I see it myself, but it's beautiful
anyway.) It was a lovely, clear night. The air was warm and still, and
the moon reflected whitely on the dark water.

Cecilia opened the car trunk and, like a magician pulling a
rabbit out of a hat, produced a fold-out picnic table with four
attached seats, as well as two other folding chairs. Boxes and bags
of food followed, as well as wine, champagne and miniature bottles
of a wonderfully bitter drink called Fernet, which is very popular
in Buenos Aires and to which I've become mildly addicted. She
whipped a Christmas cloth over the table and then — the icing on
the cake — brought out a string of multicoloured, battery-powered
fairy lights, which she proceeded to string over the tree under
which lay our holiday spread. We were ready to party!

Other revellers began to arrive, including a Brazilian family who claimed a bench beside us — we shared our extra chairs and food bounty with them.

With some time to wait before midnight, we took turns walking around the area. Taking advantage of the music coming from the waterside restaurants, Linda and I danced our way across the bridge and back. And when any of us needed to visit the washroom, we simply availed ourselves of the facilities in the nearby Hilton Hotel! (As a side note, the people in the hotel restaurant looked as if they weren't having nearly as much fun as we were!)

Gradually the excitement began to build towards midnight. Then at the stroke of twelve, 2017 was ushered in with a burst of colour and sound as fireworks erupted all around the area. The usual "oohs" and "aahs" accompanied shouts of *Feliz Año Nuevo*, and a great deal of kissing and hugging.

We from the northern hemisphere were thrilled just to be celebrating New Year outside in this balmy summer weather, but thanks to Cecilia's generosity and sense of fun, it turned out to be much more.

Jo-anne and Linda are both widely travelled, and one of them (I can't remember which) declared this the best New Year's Eve she could ever remember!

We all made noises about doing it again next year. And judging by the reactions of our many friends as well as Cecilia's family, we might have to get a bigger table!

Chapter Eleven

VENDIMIA!

Argentina boasts three wine regions: the northern provinces of Salta, Catamarca and Tucuman; the Cuyo region including La Rioja, Mendoza and San Juan; and the Neuquen, La Pampa and Rio Negro areas of Patagonia.

But the most famous is Mendoza. A two-hour flight from Buenos Aires, the city of Mendoza is the capital of Mendoza Province, which stretches out to the wine growing region of the Valle de Uco in the foothills of the Andes.

The wine harvest festival, or *La Vendimia*, takes place in the first weekend of March, and as my friends Susan and Michael were there on vacation from Ecuador, I decided to join them for the weekend. Susan, with her experience as a travel agent, arranged the whole trip, and I was duly met at the airport by our trusty driver, Jorge.

When we arrived at the hotel, my two friends were in the lobby waiting to welcome me with a giant Argentine *abrazo y beso* (hug and kiss) — a custom that endears itself to most people very quickly. I hardly had enough time to check in and change before Jorge was back, ready to whisk us all off to our first winery tour and tasting — this set the tone for the rest of my visit!

Fresh from the frenetic rush of Buenos Aires, I found Mendoza a lovely change of pace. It's a smaller city, full of trees and pure fresh air. But we were headed out of the city to Tupungato in the Valle de Uco, where our destination was the winery of Ruca Malen.

After a warm welcome, we were escorted round to the back of the building, where we gasped at the sight before us. Acres of parallel rows of grape vines stretched as far as the eye could see, with the dramatic backdrop of the snow-capped Andes on the distant horizon.

Until the other guests arrived, we were seated at a table covered with a selection of wine glasses that hinted at the delights to come.

When the tour began, I learned some new facts about wine cultivation — at least as it's done in Argentina. For instance, at the end of each row of vines is a rose bush. Not just there for their beauty, these play an important role. Rosebushes are susceptible to some of the same pests as grapevines, so when mildew is found on the rosebushes the vines are immediately sprayed to prevent infection and keep them healthy.

As she escorted us around the kitchen garden, the owner proudly told us it supplied all the vegetables served in the restaurant.

Next came the wine production building, with its massive vats of wine at various stages of maturation. By this time, though, we were eager to try the previous contents of the vats, and we were also getting hungry.

Back to the wineglass-laden table we went, even more appreciative now of the serene beauty of the vines.

We were presented with the menu, a thing of beauty in itself, which described in glowing gastronomical terms a series of five — yes five — food courses, each with its selection of wine. I wish I had kept the menu, as I don't remember the dishes, but they were all very exotic, like nothing I'd eaten before and all scrumptious.

And the wine! Ah yes, those delectable liquid jewels! We decided to keep track of our preferences and vote for our favourites, but by the time we'd finished we couldn't choose a favourite because they were all wonderful.

We rolled out of Ruca Malen, sated with both food and wine, but we weren't done yet. Jorge, a native of Tupungato, said we couldn't miss a visit to the local ice cream shop.

Argentines love their ice cream, and no wonder. Despite our groaning stomachs, we managed to do justice to this fine example of local artisanal food.

On arriving back at our hotel, not surprisingly we all opted for a nap.

———

Next day, Saturday, was the big day. On this day the regional beauty queens would parade through the city in beautiful carriages, accompanied by handsome *gauchos* on magnificent horses. Then the Queen of the *Vendimia* would be crowned at the spectacular show at night.

As a modern North American woman, I'm not a fan of beauty pageants as a rule, but everyone was so caught up in this whole event that it would have been churlish not to join in the fun. Certainly the young women seemed very excited about it all, and there was a certain innocence about it that made it very appealing.

We thought we'd have coffee on a patio on the main street but, knowing this was prime real estate for the parade, they insisted we have lunch instead. So we happily settled in for an early lunch — which went on until mid-afternoon!

The parade was a rather informal affair — I didn't see any marshals or anybody who appeared to be in charge at all. Carriage after carriage rolled past, graced by not only the queens but also their attendants, both male and female. They threw flowers, and we laughingly caught them. They danced to folkloric music from their regions, and we smiled and moved to the beat.

But my favourite part was the gauchos and their beautiful horses. Not only adults, but boys and girls as young as about nine

sat atop huge muscular horses, holding them perfectly under
control even during long pauses
in the movement. Amazing!

Susan, an intrepid and highly
skilled photographer, kept disap-
pearing to capture images that
would perfectly represent these
memorable moments.

Eventually, around 3 pm, we
wandered back to our hotel for a
nap before the main event —
The Show!

Susan's photograph of a little Gaucho.
Isn't he adorable?

The highlight of the *Vendimia* weekend is a spectacular show held
in a huge amphitheatre outside the city. Getting tickets isn't easy,
but clever Susan had managed to snag three for us.

Like most entertainment in Argentina, this show started late
— around 10 p.m. We were picked up in a minibus at our hotel and
carried to the venue shortly after six. I don't know why we had to
be there so early and we had a lot of waiting around to do, but it
was fun watching the huge stage go through its lighting and prepa-
ration, while people watched and chatted. My only concern was
that I might have to find a washroom in this vast, people-filled
place. Fortunately, all our bladders held up, so that wasn't a
problem.

The tour company had provided each of us with a "packed
lunch". I've had prepackaged meals before, but never one that
included a half bottle of Malbec and a piccolo of champagne! No
doubt about it, Argentines know how to live.

Finally, just a little later than the posted showtime, the excitement reached fever pitch. The music started, all the lights dimmed
except those over the massive stage — and in a burst of colour,
energy and exuberance, 900 singers and dancers erupted onto the

stage! (I know there were 900 because I counted their names on the program next day.)

What a spectacle! The show was a mix of vignettes of events in Argentine history, folkloric dancing and even tango, and — unfortunately — speeches. I guess local politicians are the same all over the world — they love to talk!

Eventually, the long-awaited choosing of the Queen of the *Vendimia* arrived. None of us was quite clear about the voting process, but judging by the volume of applause, the winner was a popular choice.

And finally — around 2.30 am — the show ended with more spectacular singing and dancing, culminating in fireworks and dancing by the crowd, including Susan, Michael and me!

As we trudged along the dirt road back to our bus we all agreed we wouldn't have missed this for the world. I was a happy girl as I fell into bed that night, with the sounds and sights of *La Vendimia* swirling in my head.

Up bright and early next day, I still had one more full day in Mendoza, although Susan and Michael would be there for a bit longer. We decided to spend it on — you guessed it — another winery tour!

On our way there, we noticed a huge statue of Christ high up in the mountains. On hearing us mention it, Jorge made a sharp turn onto an upward track — nothing would do but we would see the statue up close.

Cristo Rey del Valle

Although the scenery was magnificent, the ride was hair-raising. I imagine lots of tourists direct earnest prayers at the statue — gratitude for getting up safely and petitions for a safe descent!

The winery of the day was called Salentein. Quite a new winery, its location nestled in the foothills of the Andes is a fairytale setting.

Salentein Winery, Valle de Uco

We weren't given food here, but instead we had a useful lesson in wine tasting with more detail than at the other wineries. I now understand that at least some of the posturing by would-be "connoisseurs" is a load of old rubbish!

Deep down in the wine cellars we found a delightful surprise — a grand piano! Around a circular platform was a row of seats, where you can lean back against the wine barrels and listen to music. Isn't that a cool idea? Unfortunately, there was no concert while we were there, so we could only imagine the beautiful acoustics the place has.

On the way back, we discovered that grapes are not the only produce pressed into delicious service in Mendoza, when Jorge took us to a local olive processing factory. There we dipped chunks of homemade bread into plain and flavoured olive oils. In the shop, I bought some lovely olive oil soap that made my skin glow.

My flight back to Buenos Aires was late next day, but I was instructed by Susan to pack and be ready to leave early. She explained that that would give us time for yet another winery tour before going to the airport!

Our third and last tour was of Gaia, the winery of the Bousquet Estate, famous for its organic wines. After the tour, sitting in the restaurant waiting for the tasting, we were offered a choice: four courses or six! By now our stomachs were begging for mercy, so we settled for four amazing plates, including dessert, each accompanied by its own glass of wonderful wine. I think this photo of Susan and me says it all!

Please, no more!

If you come to Argentina, try to time your visit to include Mendoza during the first week of March so that you can experience this gastronomical delight for yourself.

Chapter Twelve

POLO!

Argentina is universally acknowledged as the world capital of polo. Polo is not known as the sport of kings for nothing, as it's generally played and enjoyed by the rich and privileged. It's one of the two sporting passions of Argentina, the other being *futbol*, but the two are worlds apart at the opposite ends of society.

Quite a few Argentines have told me they'd never seen a polo match because that was only for the rich, and they couldn't afford it.

However...

One day in February, my friend Venetia, who is always tapped into what's going on, told me we could go to one of the first games of the season — free! I invited Cecilia and Venetia invited her friend Raul, and the four of us set off for our polo adventure. A quick glance at the Campo Argentino de **Polo** in Palermo tells you it would normally be surrounded by expensive cars — but we arrived on the No. 10 bus!

On entering the main gate, the first thing we saw was a splendid statue of a polo player on horseback, mallet at full swing and leaning down towards an unseen ball. It was beautiful, and even more intriguing because it was constructed of thousands of bits of machinery, old gears and chains.

We didn't linger, as it had begun to drizzle, and we weren't sure there would even be a match. I've been told they don't play polo in the rain because it's dangerous for the horses — or maybe it's to protect the finery of the crowd.

Wonderful sculpture made out of old gears!

There are two fields in the complex, and we had a look at the main one first. The first thing I noticed was the huge size of the field — green, manicured grass surrounded by earthen tracks. On one side was the stadium, the other the Buenos Aires skyline. Very impressive.

Our game was to be played on the secondary field, and as we wandered over there the rain fortunately stopped. Game on!

We joined the small crowd in the stadium and waited expectantly. A pre-game practice began on the field, and we had our first look at the magnificent horses and their proud riders as they casually went through their moves. There's nothing quite like a big, handsome man on a big, handsome horse!

The field cleared, save for one rider who stood at the edge of the field near the timekeeper. A woman dressed in a poncho, long blonde hair flowing from beneath a very rakish gaucho hat, stood chatting to him for a few moments, before he rode off to join the other players. Maybe she was a groupie.

A bell rang — the old fashioned kind you ring by waggling the bell pull — and the game was underway. I'm sure there are lots of rules and technicalities but, like *futbol*, it's a game easily followed and enjoyed even if you don't know the rules.

With four players on each team and one umpire, it struck me again how large the field was for just nine horses. There's lots of galloping up and down the field, and the expression "thundering hooves" certainly applied.

Time after time, eight mallets swung high over the riders' heads and then swooped down to attack the ball. All the players competed for the same small space, and all at breakneck speed. It looked terrifying!

Someone stood atop the scoreboard — a huge, old-school black panel — and changed the white numbers manually as goals were scored. Tradition dies hard in Argentina, and that's a good thing.

The game ended in a victory for the home team, which always makes for a good atmosphere as the crowd disperses after any sporting event, although I think polo is such a civilized world that a winning opposition would be accorded a polite tribute too.

With the game over, it was now about 5.30 pm — time for *merienda*. This is one of those very Argentine customs everyone, visitors and locals alike, loves. Because Argentines eat dinner very late — often after 10 pm — they need sustenance in late afternoon. That's when you'll see the cafes full of people drinking coffee and eating pastries, or maybe drinking a glass of wine. On a hot summer afternoon, I usually opt for the wine!

On this particular day, Venetia had heard there was an international food truck fair at La Rural, a large outdoor facility where they hold agricultural fairs and such. So we hopped on the *colectivo* and went. After a wander round to examine the international goodies on hand, I settled for an *arepa*, a light corn sandwich native to Venezuela, and some of the sweet Argentine cider. As a live band played ear-splitting rock music in the background, conversation was impossible and we gave all our attention to the food — and, of course, the people-watching.

As Cecilia and I had been invited to a party with some of her friends, she and I headed straight there after our meal.

Polo, food truck *merienda*, house party with local friends — this was one of those lovely days when I truly felt like an Argentine!

Chapter Thirteen

RAIN!

It was Saturday, and I had been invited to two possible events for the evening. Instead of choosing between them, I decided to do both.

Buenos Aires International Newcomers (BAIN) is my favourite of the expat/travellers organizations, because its members are from around the world, including some from right here in Argentina. It was "wine and tapas night", an event held monthly at a member's home.

There was also an open air *milonga* being held at the Centro Cultural Kirchner, a wonderful old building that was once the city's main post office and is now used for a wide array of cultural activities — amazingly, many of them free. The *milonga* was to start at 4 pm, so I planned to go there around 5 pm (nobody wants to be there first!), stay for a couple of hours and then head out to the BAIN event.

Just as I was arriving at the CCK it was starting to spit rain, and the *milonga* had been moved inside. It was a lovely space though, and there was an excellent live orchestra.

Other than at larger concerts and shows, a tango orchestra is small, usually with a violinist, a pianist, sometimes a guitarist. But the most important instrument, the one that gives tango music that heart rending melancholy, is the bandoneon. It looks similar to an accordion or concertina, but the sound is unique.

I sat with an Argentine couple, danced a few *tandas* and generally had a good time.

At 7.30 pm, as planned, I prepared to leave. When I arrived at the front door and looked out, it was as if the entrance had turned into a wall of water! The rain was so heavy you couldn't see drops at all — just a deluge.

I stepped back inside and delved into my tote bag, which I had packed quite thoughtfully. In the bottom were my wine and tapas for BAIN. In case it turned cool (which it didn't), I had put in a shawl. Thinking it might possibly rain (!), I had thrown in my stylish red rain poncho. And on top of it all were my precious tango shoes in their own bag.

I struggled into the poncho. I stepped outside. The poncho blew off. By the time I got it on again I was already soaked, but I persevered.

The bus to the wine and tapas event was across the street, so I leaned forward and pushed over there through wind and rain, several times almost bumping into others doing the same thing.

The bus was missing in action, and after ten minutes I decided I'd better get a taxi. Hah! Everybody else had the same idea, and we all stood in the blinding rain, hailing taxis that were already filled to capacity. I quickly realized I couldn't show up at somebody's home in this state, dripping all over the floor, and I should just take a taxi home. But what taxi? This was getting ridiculous.

Eventually, I saw the trusty 152 bus emerging from the rain and I hopped on that instead — everybody else was dripping too but so glad to be out of the rain we were all smiling. Very Buenos Aires!

I had a good ten-minute walk from the bus stop, and I felt as if

I was swimming down the street. If you've ever seen the classic movie "Singing In the Rain", just picture that scene with Gene Kelly dancing down the street in the rain and you'll have some idea of how it was! There was no point to rain gear by this time. My hair was plastered to my head and my clothes were clinging to my body. The great thing, though, was that it wasn't cold.

The drainage system in Buenos Aires is not what it might be, and to cross the road I had to step in puddles literally up to my ankles. It's a miracle my sandals survived.

At last I turned the key in the front door of my building — only to find the elevators were not working! At this point I just had to laugh. I fished my iPhone with its flashlight out of my purse and started up the stairs to my apartment — on the eighth floor!

I can read in the dark — no problem!

I had been through a power outage a few weeks earlier, and had equipped myself with a flashlight, which I quickly found. I had my Kindle, so I could read in the dark, and somewhere in the dark kitchen I had a bottle of Malbec — I always have a bottle of Malbec. I peeled off my wet clothes and settled into the couch to read. This wasn't so bad!

After creeping around in the dark for half an hour or so, I suddenly noticed there were lights on my modem. Hmm. I must have Internet. On a whim, I switched on a lamp — all the lights came on! Turns out there wasn't a general power outage, just the elevators and the lights in the stairwell. Oh well, no problem here at all.

Until next morning. No water!

The water system in the building is electrically driven, and the previous night's rain had poured into places it shouldn't. There was enough left in the tank for a very sparse, dribbly, lukewarm shower but that was it. So down the eight flights of spiral stairs in the dark I went, picked up four large bottles of water and climbed back up.

This went on for two days before the water and the elevators came back on at the same time — hallelujah!

These heavy rains and flash floods are not unusual in Buenos Aires, and the people are quite sanguine about it. Now that I know what to expect, I just accept it too.

And after all, beautiful Buenos Aires is worth a little inconvenience!

Chapter Fourteen

OCEAN!

For me, the only negative about Buenos Aires is that it's not on the ocean. Yes, it is on the mouth of the Rio de la Plata, which is so wide it looks like the ocean, but it's not. Every so often I have a yen to go to the beach — a long, sandy ocean beach with the waves lapping at my feet.

There are several places Porteños go to indulge themselves with beach holidays. One of the most popular is Punta Del Este, which is not in Argentina at all, but across the river in Uruguay.

But if you want to stay in Argentina, just head southeast from Buenos Aires and drive for four or five hours. You'll come to several towns that offer great beaches, probably the most popular of which is Mar Del Plata. It is, however, SO popular that during the height of the summer it can be almost impossible to get reservations at the good restaurants when the tourist population explodes.

I wanted to see it without competing with thousands of other visitors for a patch on the beach, so Cecilia suggested we go for a few days at the end of the season. We planned our trip for early March, and Cecilia's friends Flora and Carlos invited us to stay with them in their lovely condo overlooking the ocean.

As we wanted to have as much of the day in Mar Del Plata as possible, we decided to leave very early in the morning and arrive around lunch time. So I was bleary-eyed and still half asleep when Cecilia picked me up at 5 am. It was, of course, still dark, and Buenos Aires looked quite different as we took the highway out of the city. We were treated to a spectacular sunrise, deep mauves and purples turning to red and gold as the day began.

After a couple of hours on the road, I was beginning to get hungry. Reading my mind, Cecilia said we would stop soon for breakfast at a place she knew well, where she promised me the best *medialunas* I'd ever tasted. That got my taste buds standing to attention!

Sure enough, passing the sign for Chas-comús, we pulled into an old-time roadside diner called Atalaya. Its huge parking lot was already filling up — this was clearly one of those places that has been around for a very long time and is well known to all who travel this stretch of highway. The smell of freshly baked *medialunas* greeted us as we opened the door, and my appetite went up another couple of notches.

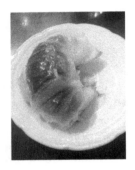

Mmmmmmm!

It's basically one large room filled with tables and chairs, nothing fancy. The waiters don't need order pads here, as the menu is simple: coffee and *medialunas*. And what *medialunas* they were! Soft, buttery and still warm from the oven. We each ate two right there and took more with us for the road!

Are you wondering if we had an *aventura* on this trip? Oh yes, we did.

Soon after breakfast, we took a little detour so that I could see a lovely little lake off the main road. To make sure we found our way back to the highway, Cecilia rolled down the passenger side window and asked someone for directions. When we'd been back on the road for ten minutes or so, I started to feel a bit chilly and realized the window was halfway down. When I pressed the button to close it, nothing happened. Cecilia tried from her side — nothing. We pulled over to the roadside, but when Cecilia tried to force it closed it rolled down to full open, and nothing we could do would close it again!

We were an hour or so away from Castelli, where we figured we could get it fixed. I moved into the back seat and pulled Cecilia's spare jacket over my head and shoulders as the wind blasted in from the highway. It was a chilly drive, but what the heck, it was an *aventura!*

Castelli is a strange little town. It seemed like almost all houses — no sign of stores or offices. For some reason, there were police officers on several of the corners — even though there was little traffic and we didn't see anyone walking. We asked one for directions to the nearest auto repair shop, and although we followed them to the letter we never did find the place he told us about. So we asked another policeman, got more directions to a different place, and after much crawling along at low speed to minimize the wind, we found it.

But it didn't do us much good, as the mechanic took a look at the problem and said it would take him a whole day to fix it. We found yet another place and they couldn't do it at all because they were too busy. There must have been more going on in Castelli than met the eye!

So we decided that since we had managed thus far with the window open, we might as well carry on to Mar Del Plata and get it fixed there. I wrapped myself up as best I could again, and off we went. We had called Flora from the road to tell her what had happened, and she had called her regular mechanic and arranged for us to take the car there. So my first glimpse of the famous Mar Del Plata beach playground was an auto mechanic's shop off the main drag! But I shouldn't complain, because they fixed the door in ninety minutes while we went for a stroll in the sun to bring our body temperatures back up to normal!

I love to read other people's travel stories, and I've noticed that real travellers always try to get to know the local people wherever they are. It's not always easy to do that, and I'm particularly gratified that on my first four visits I've been entertained in the homes of quite a number of Argentines. Many of those contacts have come as a result of my friendship with Cecilia. Whenever I mention travelling to a new part of Argentina, Cecilia invariably replies, "I have a friend there....". Mar Del Plata was no exception.

After the car was repaired, it was time for lunch. At Flora's suggestion, we went to a local restaurant that catered to the folks who lived around there rather than the gazillion tourists who flood the more well known places throughout the summer months. We were joined by Flora's husband Carlos and enjoyed some yummy pasta.

Rocky shore at Mar Del Plata!

Then Carlos gave us a tour of Mar Del Plata. I have always loved the sea, and it is certainly a prominent feature of this town. I particularly liked the contrast between the manicured beaches, with their rows of bathing cabañas, and their rugged rocky counterparts just a little way down the road. When I see rocks like those, my inner child comes out and wants to clamber over them as I did on childhood vacations!

Flora pointed out a restaurant right down by the beach, nestled into the edges of the rocks, and I was delighted to hear we would be going there for dinner that night.

When we arrived with Flora, Carlos and their daughter Maria, I was surprised to see we had the room almost to ourselves. As Flora said, though, the summer season was all but over. Apparently if we had come a few weeks earlier we wouldn't have been able to get a table!

The restaurant was positioned in such a way that we seemed to be suspended over the ocean, inky black now except for the silvery moonlight picking out the white waves. It was enchanting.

———

My favourite memory of Mar Del Plata, though, came the following evening. I was sitting on the couch in our friends' apartment reading, when I heard the soft sounds of guitar music coming from another room. When I went to investigate, I found Carlos sitting quietly playing his guitar and singing softly to himself. With a little encouragement, he brought the music into the living room and entertained us all while Flora cooked dinner.

After dinner, as we sat around the table, a little spontaneous singalong developed. They sang songs I didn't know, but hummed along anyway. In Scotland, where I was born, it seems as if everyone loves to sing, and I grew up with this sort of entertainment. It was lovely to experience it on the other side of the world, in a totally different environment. Music truly is the universal language!

———

I'm not sure how the rest of our planned visit would have unfolded, because sometime during the night I suddenly found myself quite sick, so much so that I readily agreed with Cecilia's suggestion that we go home a day early. A visit to the hospital in Buenos Aires told me I had contracted pneumonia, and I was out of commission for a couple of weeks.

Naturally, this rather took the edge off my seaside adventure, but it just means one thing — I'll have to go back to Mar Del Plata sometime soon!

Chapter Fifteen

FLAG!

I was invited to visit Cecilia's sister Adriana in Rosario for a few days. She had been visiting Buenos Aires, and this would be a combination of driving her home and having a chance to see another place I hadn't visited before. Of course I accepted the invitation, although I'm bound to admit I didn't really think Rosario would hold much of interest. Happily, I was wrong.

Rosario is a city of almost two million people in the province of Santa Fe in central Argentina. It's about 300 kilometres northeast of Buenos Aires, so about a half-day's drive. Although the guidebooks will tell you the drive is along the Paraná River, in truth you don't see much of the river until you are almost there.

Although we could probably have waited till we arrived, we decided to stop along the way for lunch at one of the many *parilllas* on the highway. Now I don't know about you, but I think of these stops as a time to grab a quick bite, maybe a sandwich and a coffee. But these ladies are Argentine, and they were ready to eat properly!

When you order the full *parilla* in a restaurant, it comes to your table on its own little grill, which keeps the food hot until you eat it. Although I would have just ordered a snack, I must admit my mouth watered when I saw and smelled the selection of beef, lamb, chicken and sausages. Good choice!

In our conversation, I mentioned that I had brought my sketching materials, and they both said Rosario had "a monument" I could sketch. As Buenos Aires is chock full of monuments, this didn't sound like anything special. Again, Rosario surprised me, as this is no ordinary monument.

One of the city's major claims to fame is as the birthplace of the national flag of Argentina. The flag was designed by Manuel Belgrano, who raised it for the first time on an island in the river in 1812, during the War of Independence.

I love the Argentine flag. It's different from the usual bright, strident primary colours of most national flags in that its horizontal bands are a lovely shade of light blue, and on the white middle band sits what's known as the "Sun of May" in reference to the May Revolution.

The monument my friends were referring to is the National Flag Memorial, or in Spanish *Monumento Histórico Nacional a la Bandera*. And what a monument it is! It's so big that when they pointed it out to me as we drove into town, it didn't register right away that the *whole thing* was the monument! Let me try to describe it.

Now that's what I call a monument!

The first thing that struck me was its vast size. Apparently the whole complex, because that's what it is, is about 10,000 square metres, which is basically a city block. The tower at the front is huge all by itself — I think they told me it is about 70 metres high. It's surrounded by beautiful sculptures of angels and historic figures, and heroic quotations sculpted into the lovely yellow stone, which came from the Andes. Manuel Belgrano is actually buried under this tower.

But when you walk around the side, you find there's more!

First, there's a wide open courtyard surrounded by flags. Interestingly, these flags don't have the sun on the middle band, and when I asked about this, Cecilia explained this version is known as the Ornamental Flag, and it always has to be flown below the Official Ceremonial Flag. Apparently this was the original version, so I guess it's appropriate that it gets lots of play in the memorial.

Walking across the sloping paved area, I climbed up the steps to an area called the Triumphal Propylaeum. Inside I found this

beautiful eternal flame over the tomb of the unknown warrior.
Very moving.

The monument is so massive that you
can't help seeing it from whatever direction
you arrive. It was particularly beautiful at
night, illuminated top to bottom in blue
stripes, symbolizing the colours of the flag.
Wonderful!

Tomb of the Unknown
Warrior

Rosario is the birthplace not only of the national flag, but also of
world famous football player Lionel Messi. In the vicinity of the
monument is a cafe which I understand belonged either to him or
to someone in his family. We had coffee there, but I didn't see any
sign of the famous feet.

In our explorations next day, Cecilia took me to a square
commemorating another of Rosario's native sons, the revolu-
tionary Che Guevara. It wasn't very impressive, to tell the truth,
and it might be that the city is ambivalent about this particular
citizen. Like many other Argentine historical figures, Che Guevara
has his fans and his detractors. (He was very handsome though,
and I'm convinced that's one reason for the continuing popularity
of the iconic photo of him that still shows up on tee-shirts and
other memorabilia!)

Much more interesting, though, was our visit to a well known
cafe in downtown Rosario called Bar El Cairo. (In Argentina the
cafes all sell alcohol, so the terms 'bar' and 'cafe' are pretty much
interchangeable.)

Like many of the cafes in Buenos Aires, El Cairo looks much

the way it probably did in its heyday during the 1940s, and as usual I felt as if I had melted into a bygone age. El Cairo describes itself as a 'literary cafe', and this is supported by the bookshelves at the back of the room, and a small stage that's still used for readings and other performances.

But despite their old-world ambience, these cafes and bars are very much alive and well, and El Cairo is no exception. It was late morning when we arrived, and it was buzzing with people having morning coffee, or even something stronger.

El Cairo pays homage to yet another famous son of Rosario, Roberto Fontanarossa, popularly known as **El Negro**. He was a prolific writer, with a body of work that included comic short stories as well as novels. He was also well known for his cartoons, some of which are on the wall behind El Cairo's little stage.

Only actors welcome at this table!

As a regular patron of El Cairo, Fontanarossa had his own table. When we were there, although the place was busy, nobody was at that table, and Cecilia explained why. Fontanarossa was often to be found in the company of artists of various kinds, including actors. I'm not sure if he stipulated this or whether it was the current bar owners, but the only people allowed to sit at his table now are actors. Isn't that cool?

Downtown Rosario boasts amazing architecture that rivals even Buenos Aires. I almost tripped over my own feet gazing up at the beautiful buildings in the centre of town. I had been in several branches of the shopping chain Falabella in Buenos Aires, but they paled in comparison to the Rosario branch. When I walked down this lovely staircase I felt as if I was descending to greet my guests at a fabulous party!

Maybe you're wondering if we had an adventure in Rosario. Well I'll give you a hint — Cecilia was there! So of course we had to do something that turned out other than expected.

A staircase fit for a queen!

The day before we were leaving to go back to Buenos Aires, we had been out and about enjoying Rosario. It was already mid-afternoon when Cecilia and Adriana had a confab in the car and decided we should go to Victoria. When I asked where that was they waved vaguely and said "across the bridge". Have you ever noticed that when you ask a local for directions in a strange place, they always make it sound closer than it is?

They explained that Victoria was in the neighbouring province of Entre Rios, "just across the river". In fact, as I later discovered, it's about 60 kilometres away, across a number of bridges, aqueducts and earth-filled raised sections of road, on the other side of the Paraná River. It's a beautiful drive, especially crossing the high bridge and looking down on the little islands in the Delta.

We arrived in Victoria, parked the car and set off for a wander. I discovered that, like Buenos Aires, Victoria has a plaza dedicated to the great Libertador, José de San Martin. I am kind of fascinated by San Martin, so I was happy to pay homage to him in this lovely square.

By this point it had started to rain, not heavily but enough that we decided to find a cafe and have a coffee until the rain stopped. But just when we found a place, Cecilia looked up at the suddenly lowering sky and decided we should get back on the road right away and never mind the coffee — which made me a bit nervous.

Only after we were on the road did they tell me that this area was on the flood plain of the Paraná Delta, and in fact it had experienced heavy flooding just the previous week! Just about that point the rain turned much heavier. Apparently the gods were laughing at us again.

Coming from the Victoria end, we were mainly on the earth-filled sections of the road. Sometimes there were fields on either side, many home to beautiful horses, but often we were crossing an elevated section of road over a wide expanse of water. By now it was late afternoon. On our left it was full daylight as you would expect at that time of day, but on our right the sky had turned almost black, and in fact it looked like night. Weird!

My Argentine friends didn't seem overly concerned, so I soon stopped worrying too and just enjoyed the adventure. In fact, we came to no harm and soon arrived back in Rosario — where there was no rain at all and we were once again in full daylight!

I would like to go back to Victoria, as it is an attractive city with some interesting buildings. I might pay attention to the weather forecast next time.

Chapter Sixteen

DELTA!

Most visitors to Buenos Aires find their way to Tigre, which is about 28 kilometres north of the city. On my first visit, it was almost the end of my trip before I got there.

As I've mentioned before, on that first trip I was Cecilia's client for her guide business, and we hadn't yet become the fast friends we are today. A day in Tigre was part of the package, but to my puzzlement she kept putting it off and I couldn't understand why.

As I've said before, it rains in Buenos Aires, often just for an hour or so, but it can be quite heavy for that short time. Each time we planned to head for Tigre, Cecilia would tell me we couldn't go because it had rained, and we needed a few completely dry days in a row. It turns out that the reason for this concern is that Tigre is on the Paraná Delta, which is part of the flood plain that spans several Argentine provinces. Little islands are connected by small tributaries of the Rio Paraná and the Rio de la Plata, and until the rains have been absent for a couple of days, quite a bit of Tigre is underwater!

Conditions were finally right about two days before I left, and off we went. You can get to Tigre by train, but for our first visit Cecilia drove. I'll talk about the trains in a moment, but I will say that going by car gives you more scope because the places of interest are fairly far apart and involve quite a bit of walking.

We arrived just before lunch time, and headed straight for the landing stage to catch one of the many water buses, or *lanchas colectivas*. These are barge-type mahogany boats, the interior laid out exactly like a bus. We were lucky enough to get seats by the window so that I could get the best views.

The *lanchas* pick up passengers at the islands, many of which are populated by a combination of year-round inhabitants and summer visitors. The decision to stop at any one of them seemed to be simply someone standing on the dock waving! We were headed for an island called *Tres Bocas*, which meant we had about a half-hour trip on the water.

Island of Tres Bocas, Tigre

It's very scenic, with lots of lush greenery on all sides as the boat meanders through the islands. Some have beaches — not the manicured variety you find in large resorts, but simply the sandy edge of the land. I had to laugh when Cecilia pointed at one island and said, "That is a beautiful beach, but it's not there today." She wasn't kidding. This is what happens when there's been a bit of rain — pieces of the islands are submerged until the water goes back down!

We duly disembarked at *Tres Bocas*, and began our walk along the path by the water. This is a busy tourist area, so we had lots of company. (Because of the humid atmosphere there were also lots of mosquitoes!) People are very friendly, and we chatted with a number of them before arriving at Cecilia's favourite restaurant, El Horno.

The name means the oven, and its outdoor kitchen was the source of the delicious aromas that met us before we even sat down. I don't normally eat a big lunch, but I knew before we began that this would be an exception. The delights of the *parilla* kept us busy for over an hour, before we walked some of the calories off further along the river path.

For my first visit, Cecilia had pre-booked a private *lancha* for the trip back to the mainland. It wasn't as glamorous as it sounds, but I really enjoyed the different view of the area. The owner took us down "paths" between islands that were too small for the bigger boats, with many stories of past and present inhabitants (information that would definitely not be found in the guidebooks!)

———

Tigre Museum of Art

Our next destination was the most beautiful art gallery I've ever seen. I don't mean in terms of the content, but the building itself. It's called the *Museo de Arte Tigre*, and was built in the early 1900s. Somehow I had the idea it was formerly a hotel, but no, one of the helpful staff explained that it was always a museum although it had undergone some renovations in recent years. The architecture is Bel Epoque, and I think it actually warrants two visits — one to see the art and one just for the building.

One artist I discovered there was Benito Quinquela Martin. If you've ever seen those brightly coloured paintings of port scenes in La Boca, they're probably by Quinquela Martin. He specialized in these scenes of the area where he was born and grew up, and he infused them with not only strong, vibrant colours but also a sense of drama and life. I find it hard to take my eyes off them. There's a museum in La Boca dedicated to his work, and I haven't seen it yet. That's definitely on my list for A5, but in the meantime I was very happy to feast my eyes on his paintings in the Tigre gallery.

One place that's always listed in guidebook descriptions of Tigre is the *Puerto de Frutas*, the Fruit Market, so called because it used to *be* a fruit market. Today, you'll find a wide selection of goods for sale there — but no fruit! On Eleanore's visit, she and I spent a day in Tigre with Cecilia and we had an excellent lunch in the *Puerto de Frutas*, but the market itself wasn't particularly appealing. There were some crafts places, but there seemed to be more household goods and lots of baskets, many made in China.

I've mentioned this before, but Argentines love ice cream. You can enjoy the frozen treat after midnight in many of the specialty shops in Buenos Aires, and most people have their favourites. But I've heard more than one person say the best ice cream shop on the planet it is Tigre, and I wouldn't argue! It's called Via Toscana, and if you have trouble finding it just ask anyone you meet, because *everyone* knows where it is.

You enter through a delightful little garden courtyard, which is usually populated by people enjoying gigantic cones — you have to sit down to savour these as they deserve all your attention. When I first saw the tiny cones I was tempted to have the large size, but fortunately Cecilia warned me against that. The size of the cone is no indication of the amount of ice cream you get, as they skillfully shape your chosen flavours into a tower of deliciousness such as you'll see nowhere else!

The variety is so wide it usually takes folks quite a while to decide, and they're quite willing to let you sample freely before you buy. On the days I was there the flavours included avocado with cream and carrot cream, as well as the usual vanilla and *dulce de leche*. Put aside some pesos in your budget for this as it's not cheap, but well worth it. Via Toscana is definitely on my list every time I visit Tigre!

———

While it's always nice to have company, one day I decided to take the trip to Tigre on my own. When I go to Cecilia's home in Olivos, I take the Tigre train, so it was simple to just stay on till the end of the line. It takes about an hour, and as I've said before, you may be entertained by many of the itinerant musicians or inventive sellers of wares during the trip.

There's another way of getting there by train, called the *Tren de la Costa*. I haven't taken this one yet, but I've been told it's a great way to enjoy a leisurely half-day journey. That's because it stops at eleven points along the way, and you can get off and on again at any of them. This is another item on my list for A5.

I took the Mitre train from Retiro, and arrived just before lunchtime. As I walked off the train and into the station, I was surprised to hear the distinctive sound of tango music, so I gravitated towards the small crowd that had gathered. A couple of young *tangueros* was giving a demonstration as good as anything I've seen in the tango shows of Buenos Aires! The crowd was enthralled with their flying feet and serious expressions, and they were rewarded with willing donations at the end.

On this visit I decided not to take the water bus, but rather one of the many cruise boats. It's worth checking all of these out before choosing, as there's quite a difference in price. I chose a 1-hour catamaran cruise, and as I was one of the first on board I got a great seat with a clear view. Although there's lots to see all along the way, one of my favourite sites is the Sarmiento House.

Sarmiento House

Domingo Sarmiento was the 7th President of Argentina, and he lived in this house for about thirty years until his death in 1888. An old wooden house like this might not survive well in the damp environment of Tigre, so it has been enclosed inside a glass structure to protect it. Cameras were clicking furiously on the boat as we passed this highly unusual building!

Each time I go to Argentina I think I won't bother with Tigre this time, but its watery surroundings keep drawing me back.

Chapter Seventeen

SIMPLY COOL PLACES!

ARTISAN MARKETS

If you love craft markets, where artisans gather to sell a wide variety of beautiful — and, let's be honest, sometimes not so beautiful — handmade items, you'll have lots of choice in Buenos Aires. Two of my favourites are Recoleta and San Telmo.

I live in Recoleta, so it didn't take long for me to discover this weekend institution, which takes place every Saturday and Sunday on the wide grassy space of Plaza Francia. It's a shopper's paradise, with artists selling everything from a wide and eclectic array of jewellery to handmade clothes, scarves, toys, leather goods and much more. There's rarely a weekend when I don't spend at least a half hour or so there, often much longer. I even did my Christmas shopping one year!

The San Telmo craft market takes place every Sunday, and is even bigger than Recoleta. As there's no green space big enough, the market simply takes over Defensa, one of the main streets of the barrio. Conveniently, after looking and buying your fill of amazing things, you'll emerge at Plaza Dorrego, where you can see lovely displays of tango while you eat lunch at an outdoor cafe.

While the Recoleta market is lovely, if you want a taste of authentic *Porteño* culture with your shopping, I'd choose San Telmo. This is one of the oldest barrios in Buenos Aires, and much of the original architecture is still in active use. If you are a sketcher or photographer, San Telmo offers a rich source of material.

EL CEMENTERIO DE LA RECOLETA

Cemeteries are not usually on my sightseeing list, but this one is an exception. The rich and famous of Argentina have been laid to rest here for generations and the names on the tombs and monuments seem strangely familiar because many have streets named after them.

Many of the august personages here are not familiar to visitors, but everyone has heard of Eva Peron and hers is one of the most visited tombs — although to be honest, there are many more impressive ones. The place is huge, so it's fortunate that they have a numbered map at the entrance, and you'll almost always find people looking for Evita. In fact, it is her family tomb, simply marked "Duarte", and when you're getting close you'll easily recognize it because there are always fresh flowers left on the door by visitors.

Recoleta Cemetery

There are no flat headstones here, or any grass. They are all mausoleums, arranged in broad avenues and narrow lanes, so it looks like a little town — except all the residents are dead!

It's a sun trap in the summer, and the tall trees do little to protect you from the blazing sun reflecting off all that stone and marble, so do remember your sunblock and your hat.

It's well worth a visit. I've been there many times and you'd think I'd have had enough, but my sketchbook won't let me stay away!

PLAZA SAN MARTIN

I've noticed an idiosyncrasy about cities in Argentina — they all have the same street names. Some are named after places, including other South American countries, but there are always a few called by the famous dates in Argentine history. Avenida 25 de Mayo, for example, marks the date in 1810 on which the Buenos Aires Council deposed the Spanish viceroy, while 9 de Julio, 1816 saw Argentina's final independence from Spain.

But many streets are named after past presidents and other

historical figures. Thus, all the places I've visited have streets called Sarmiento, Belgrano, Vicente Lopez and others.

And San Martin.

I read somewhere that all Argentina's heroes were polarizing forces, loved and hated in equal measure. Except one: General José de San Martin, *El Libertador*, who is universally revered. By liberating Argentina from Spanish rule and then going on to do the same for Peru and Chile, he earned his sobriquet honestly! He is celebrated in cities throughout Argentina with streets known as Libertador as well as San Martin. Unlike many other historical figures, though, San Martin also has a square in many cities.

Monument to General Jose de San Martin, El Libertador

Plaza San Martin in Buenos Aires is one of my favourite places to go to sketch, to wander, to sit in the shade of the many quirky trees — and to admire the magnificent monument. I'll never forget the glorious March afternoon when I made this sketch.

Since the monument must, of course, be prominent, it stands in a place separated from the shade trees, and there are no seats. So I had to sit on the hot, hard ground for an hour, the Argentine sun beating down mercilessly on my poor head. I had to wipe sweat away from my sketch to prevent the water colours from running! I reckon I paid due tribute to *El Liberator* that day!

Last November, I took my friend Pauline there. She was visiting from Canada, and I was showing her my favourite places in Buenos Aires. When we arrived, in early afternoon, we were surprised to find Plaza San Martin festooned with Argentine and Canadian flags! It turned out that Justin Trudeau, the Prime Minister of Canada, was here on a state visit, and the rolled-up red carpet told us we had just missed him. Too bad — I would like to have shaken his hand and welcomed a fellow Canadian to Argentina!

MY 'ENCHANTED FOREST'

A rich variety of trees is a prominent feature of Buenos Aires. It's a very green city, with parks and plazas liberally scattered throughout, and many little gems you just come upon when you turn an unfamiliar corner. I like trees that blossom, and the following are three favourites.

The *palo borracho* (drunken stick) has a weirdly shaped trunk, but its abundant blossoms convert many of the parks and treelined avenues into ribbons of pink clouds for the summer months. The national tree of Argentina, the *ceibo*, with its sumptuous deep red blossoms, is not quite so numerous, and definitely worth photographing when you do see one. Finally, there's the *jacaranda*, my favourite. This one blossoms in spring, and when I arrive in November they are in full bloom. They don't bloom for long, and the first time I came at that time of year I put off sketching for several days, and suddenly one morning it was too late, as the luxuriant purple flowers had given way to the more mundane green leaves.

In another chapter I talk about the ancient rubber tree outside La Biela, and those trees with their massive, gnarled root systems rising well above ground, are prolific across the city. If you come out of La Biela, cross Avenida Quintana and walk down a set of steps, you'll come to Avenida Alvear. Cross that too, and you'll come upon a little gem I call the Enchanted Forest. The magical shapes of the trees make me think of Harry Potter and the enchanted forest around Hogwarts, or the Narnia of *The Lion, the Witch and the Wardrobe.*

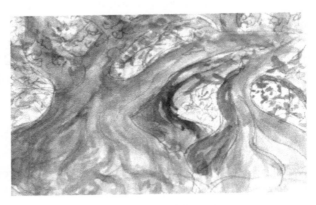

My Enchanted Forest!

The whole area — which I suppose you'd call a park — is not much bigger than a football field, and the seats scattered about let visitors relax as they gaze in wonder at those funky trees.

This is also a favourite haunt of the many professional dog walkers of Buenos Aires, and it's not unusual to see a couple of young guys or girls sitting on a tree root, surrounded by twenty or so dogs, rushing around enjoying their freedom together.

One tree has a hollow in its trunk that looks like a door into a parallel world — if I had any leanings toward fantasy I would use it in a short story. In fact, when I photographed Susan investigating the tree hollow, I told her the perfect caption for the photo would be, "And we never saw her again!"

CAMINITO

Caminito is a small area within the working class barrio of La Boca, and because people are often warned of the dangers of wandering in La Boca at night alone, sometimes they miss Caminito. That's a shame. While it's easy to take the 152 bus right there, if you're nervous you can always take a taxi, and there are lots available to take you home again.

If you've ever seen photos of Buenos Aires, you'll often see a collection of houses and other buildings with corrugated siding and painted in brilliant colours. That's Caminito.

Because La Boca is near the docks, from the earliest days it was home to dockworkers, many immigrants from Italy and Spain who were here by themselves hoping to make enough money to bring their families. The story goes that the materials and paint for their homes were leftovers from the shipyards. So if you stop to think that these poor immigrant workers were responsible for Caminito, tango and Boca Juniors, you'll realize what an impact they have had on Buenos Aires as we know and love it today.

Caminito is pretty much a tourist trap, but a fun one to spend a day in. There's a tiny square in the centre, where tango shows often spring up without warning, and several rows of artisan stands selling some beautiful jewellery and other gifts. The main street, Caminito itself, is filled with a series of outdoor eating places one after the other, several with mini tango shows going on all day to attract customers. The dancers will come around every so often to collect tips — be generous because, after all, they have entertained you.

Caminito

I've eaten in three or four of these places, and found the food to be pretty good, if expensive. Remember — tourist trap. But just the opportunity to sit in the sun and soak up the atmosphere is worth the extra pesos.

And then there are the shops. Like tourist areas around the world, they are a mixture of tatty souvenirs — including plaster statues of the Pope, who is a son of Buenos Aires and a rock star here — and beautiful high-end leather goods and lovely handmade gifts. Here I bought an authentic gaucho poncho, which I wear with pleasure during spring and fall back in Toronto. It's a real conversation starter, and has the added benefit of making me feel I'm back in Argentina!

Don't let the fearmongers scare you off. Just go during the day and stick to the main tourist centre, and you'll be just fine. And you'll have experienced one of those little gems you could never imagine in any place other than Buenos Aires.

EL ATENEO GRAND SPLENDID

I've never been in a city that so respects books and writers. On Avenida de Mayo and Avenida Corrientes, just to name two, there are stretches where you'll see one book shop after another, always with at least a few patrons browsing the tables. And these are old-school bookshops that just sell books — what a concept, eh? You might see the odd notebook or postcard in some, but none of the candles and giftware that have taken over so many of the book-shops in North America. Even though everyone has a cellphone and all the other tech toys, people here still love to read books.

On my first visit, I woke up one day to pouring rain that was clearly on for the day. Not wanting to stay in my hotel room, I went online and Googled, "what to do in Buenos Aires when it's raining". Up popped all sorts of suggestions, one of which was El Ateneo Grand Splendid. El Ateneo is a chain of bookstores, and I'd seen a few of them around but this one sounded quite special, so I jumped in a taxi and went along.

When I walked in the front door my jaw dropped — this was definitely not your average bookstore. In fact, a hundred or so years ago it was an opera house — The Grand Splendid — but in recent years it was not in use. In North America we would prob-ably knock it down and build condos, but not here. Instead, they turned it into what they claim — and I wouldn't argue — is the world's most beautiful bookstore!

Like most visitors, I stopped right inside and gasped, as I took it all in. First, I walked through the old theatre foyer, still with its tall pillars and marble stairs off to the side, but now filled with tables and shelves of books on an eclectic array of subjects. On the right is the original box office, which is now where you pay for your purchases.

Walking onto the main floor, I looked up to see the beautiful domed fresco ceiling that graced the old theatre. Instead of seats, the main floor is now full of bookshelves, carefully arranged by subject matter, and there are usually quite a few book lovers sitting on the floor perusing their potential purchases.

A first glance at the four balcony levels creates the illusion that it's still a theatre, and it's only when you look closely that you see those are not seats with people on them, but rows and rows of books.

And you know those theatre boxes right up beside the stage, usually occupied by wealthy patrons paying top price for seats? Well they're still there, but now people take books in there, and some sit for hours just reading. How utterly cool is that?

But my favourite part is the stage. They've left it in more or less its original state — curtains and all — except that it's now a cafe where you can have anything from a cup of coffee to a full course lunch with wine! I did this sketch sitting at a table onstage, surrounded by the pulleys and other theatre trappings as I worked.

I never tire of visiting this magical place, and if you come to Buenos Aires please don't miss it.

Chapter Eighteen

FAVOURITE EATING PLACES

Throughout the writing of this book I've had to keep reminding myself it's not a guidebook but a memoir of stories. I hope readers will enjoy it even if they never come to Argentina.

Having said that, I do want to talk a little about some of my favourite places and things, whether or not they're associated with *aventuras*, and that's what this chapter is about.

If you do come to Buenos Aires — and of course I think everybody should — these may give you a few ideas of where to start your own adventures.

CAFES

Buenos Aires has a cafe culture that's hard to miss. There's a plethora of cafes across the city, some on main streets and well known, others little hole-in-the-wall places hidden away where only the locals know.

I keep telling myself I don't **need** to go out for breakfast, and could just as easily eat yogurt at home, but I can never resist for more than a few days. Here are just three of the good ones you shouldn't miss.

Dos Escudos Confiteria

Dos Escudos is a small local chain of delightful cafes with bakeries attached (a match made in heaven, I always think), and I'm glad one is close to where I live in Recoleta because I love having breakfast there. A popular choice at both breakfast and *merienda* is the *medialuna*, Spanish for half-moon. These look like smaller versions of the French croissant but they taste quite different — more moist and buttery if a little less light and fluffy. One of those with a *cafe*

Dos Escudos — my breakfast spot!

doble (double size — I like a good size cup of coffee and not a thimbleful) sets me up for the day.

Medialunas are ubiquitous across Buenos Aires, and having tried them in many places, I've decided Dos Escudos has the best ones. They also give you a small glass of *agua con gas* (fizzy mineral water), as well as two tiny home-made sugar cookies which I take home for my mid-morning cup of tea.

Like almost all cafes in Buenos Aires, they have a TV mounted high on the wall, with no sound, inevitably on a sports channel and usually *futbol*. So I can always catch up on what's happening in the *Copa America* (America Cup), which is currently playing. I also like to do some of my writing over breakfast, and I'm actually writing this by hand in my little notebook as I savour my *medialuna*.

Cafe Tortoni

Cafe Tortoni is a destination cafe in the *MicroCentro*, on Avenida de Mayo. Opened in 1858, it's the oldest cafe in Buenos Aires, and quite unlike any other. In its heyday it was a hangout for intellectuals, writers, artists and even tango legend Carlos Gardel. The walls are covered with the works of these luminaries as well as photos of them enjoying coffee in Tortoni. I can easily imagine the smoke-filled atmosphere as they discussed the state of the world into the wee hours. Somehow it wouldn't surprise me a bit to see Ernest Hemingway stroll through the door to join them!

The decor is pure art deco, complete with stained glass ceilings and dark wood fittings — and the mandatory black and white checkered tile floor.

The food in Tortoni is OK, but that's not what people go for. I've occasionally eaten lunch there, but my preference is either a nice cool glass of white wine on a hot day, or a marvellous concoction they call a *submarino*. I ordered the *submarino* because I had heard Tortoni was famous for them,

Cafe Tortoni — the oldest cafe in Buenos Aires

and I can see why. They brought me a cup of steaming hot milk, and a small (maybe 3" long) bar of foil-wrapped milk chocolate in the shape of a submarine. You drop that into the milk and stir until it's melted — mmmmm! Now ***that's*** how to do hot chocolate!

Tortoni is definitely a tourist trap, as witness the fact that you usually have to line up outside until a table comes free. But it's worth the wait.

La Biela

La Biela is another Buenos Aires institution, not in the *Micro-Centro* this time but in my favourite barrio, Recoleta. In fact, it's just a five-minute walk from my apartment.

The word *biela* means "connecting rod", and I've sometimes heard it translated as "spanner". In either case, the reason for this rather strange name for a cafe is that when it opened in the 1940s it was a hangout for racing car drivers of the time, many of them well known such as Juan Manuel Fangio. In fact, outside the door of La Biela there is a life-size movable statue of Juan Galvez, another famous driver of the time, and now a popular photo opportunity for tourists. (I couldn't resist this one!)

Food is OK but not my favourite, but if you enjoy people watching, La Biela is the place to go. The inside of the restaurant is quite nice, but definitely takes second place to the large terrace when the weather is good. Here you'll find people relaxing over coffee, *merienda*, drinks or dinner, depending on the time of day. It's one of the places I often go of an evening for a glass of wine if I'm by myself, and never feel awkward.

Just like everyone else, I couldn't resist this photo opp!

The waiters all seem to have been there forever, and I certainly recognize most of them from my first visit three years ago. As in most cafes here, they are traditionally dressed, with white shirts, black pants and bow ties. The maitre d' is always in a black suit and tie, even on the hottest days of summer.

The terrace is partly shaded by the biggest tree I've ever seen. It's one of the huge rubber trees that proliferate in Buenos Aires, with massive root systems and branches that take over the areas all around. This one is over 200 years old, and apparently the oldest one in the city. I've watched people try to photograph it but the branches are so huge it puts everything into shade, so it's a challenge. During the summer there are often musicians entertaining the tourists under the tree, and I've even seen people dancing tango there. Lots of entertainment for the price of a cup of coffee!

These are three of the cafes I like best, but if you come here you'll have many, many great cafes to choose from and you'll soon find your own favourites.

PARILLAS

As every visitor knows, or soon finds out, Argentina is all about the beef. Although I'm told this is gradually changing, traditionally the cattle have grazed freely on the grasses of the wide, flat Pampas that span several provinces of Argentina. This results in tender tasty steaks that are the mainstay of the ever-present *asado*, the Argentine version of the barbecue. The word often refers to an event, typically held in someone's home, where the whole entertainment revolves around the meat.

The restaurants that specialize in these delicious steaks are called *Parillas* (pronounced 'pareeshas' in Buenos Aires Spanish). The actual grill on which they cook the meat is also called a *parilla* — I know it's confusing, but it's all yummy, so don't worry about it.

There are so many *parillas* in Buenos Aires that it would be impossible to try them all, but most of us have our favourites. Here are three of mine.

Posta Recoleta

In a short section of a street called Junin, across from the Recoleta Cemetery, is a row of restaurants with lovely outdoor patios and the tempting aroma of *asado* in the air. As they are all in friendly (I think) competition for the same customers, you have to run the gauntlet of employees standing outside, attempting to draw you into theirs. Don't be put off by this — just smile and say "no, gracias" and they won't push it.

My favourite of the restaurants on this strip is Posta Recoleta.

The first thing you'll notice is that the *parilla* itself (the grill) is on display in the window. It's always covered in a mouthwatering selection of meat, from steaks to sausages of various kinds, lamb and chicken. Take your pick — they're all excellent.

I always sit outside, surveying the passing parade as I eat. If you go on Saturdays, you can also enjoy a mini tango show, with just one couple showing off their moves on a tiny wooden 'floor' brought along for the purpose.

El Establo

When I want to eat steak somewhere outside my neighbour-hood of Recoleta, I often choose El Establo, which is at the corner of San Martin and Paraguay near the lovely Plaza San Martin.

No patio here, just a fairly plain set of rooms with crisp white table covers — and excellent steaks.

Its unprepossessing exterior wouldn't have tempted me inside if it hadn't been recommended by a friend, but now it's one of my go-to places when I fancy a steak, even if I'll be eating by myself.

La Gran Parilla del Plata

I've saved the best for last.

Situated at the corner of Peru and Chile in the quaint old barrio of San Telmo, this marvellous *parilla* is rarely called by its full name — people just call it *La Gran Parilla*. Whatever you call it, it's definitely my top favourite. I'm indebted to Venetia, who kept telling me this was the best *parilla* in Buenos Aires, and when I finally went I couldn't argue.

If you go here on your first visit to San Telmo, I suggest you take a bus or taxi to the corner of Paseo Colon and Chile and walk up the cobbled street past lots of other cafes and *parillas* where people will be enjoying the night and the music. (By the way, Porteños eat late, so don't expect many people before 9 pm and then it's just getting started!)

About a ten-minute walk will bring you to Peru, with *La Gran Parilla* on the left. The aroma of grilled beef will assail your nostrils before you even open the door!

Warning: you definitely need a reservation — I'd suggest no earlier than 9 pm — as this place gets very busy very quickly. Even tour bus groups come here, so those without a reservation are usually turned away disappointed. You could go earlier, of course, but I don't recommend it as you'd miss the buzz and excitement that makes it such fun to dine out in Buenos Aires.

Here, the decor is old-world traditional — black and white tiled floor, dark red walls with wine bottles mounted high near the ceiling. You'll be mesmerized by the place and the speedy waiters buzzing about delivering delicious food. But when the steaks come you'll have no attention for anything else!

For serious steak lovers only!

Although the salads are quite nice, they don't care much about vegetables here, and most folks seem to have a steak with a side order of french fries. I gasped the first time I saw my plate, almost completely hidden by my favourite *bife de chorizo* (nothing to do with the sausage of the same name). This is in my opinion the tastiest steak, even though many people swear by the *lomo*. In any case, they are tender, tasty and wonderful.

At the end of your meal you'll be offered a complimentary glass of either champagne or limoncello, a perfect ending to the memorable meal I've always had here.

La Gran Parilla is a place where groups of people go to eat and socialize, so it's not one I'd go to on my own. Fortunately there's always somebody ready and willing to enjoy the culinary delights of this wonderful traditional *parilla*.

EMPANADAS

Empanadas! Although they are readily available at home in Toronto now, for me the word always conjures up a little restaurant in Recoleta that has been famous for its empanadas for over 50 years. It's called *El Sanjuanino*, and you'll find it at the corner of Posadas and Callao.

Downstairs in El Sanjuanino

The atmosphere is delightfully quaint. Walls covered in old photos of past famous guests, faded Argentine flags, lovely old tiles and age-darkened beams create an old world ambience that adds another layer to the experience of eating there.

Although their other foods are fine too, it's the empanadas that draw so many locals as well as visitors. Get there early, as it fills up quickly.

ICE CREAM

I've talked about ice cream in other chapters, because it's such an integral part of life in Argentina. But there's one place that warrants special mention. It's in Olivos, where Cecilia lives, and it's called Arnaldo's.

One day I had been invited to Cecilia's for dinner, together with her family and a couple of friends. We were probably a dozen or so in all. Round about midnight, after an evening of good food, good wine and good company, someone suggested we should have ice cream. I assumed we were going to send out for it (most things can be delivered in Buenos Aires) but no, this was going to be an outing!

We piled into several cars and arrived at Arnaldo's about fifteen minutes later, as it took time to find parking spots even at this hour.

Given the hour, I had expected a couple of servers waiting sleepily for business, but boy was I wrong! The place was jumping! I joked with Cecilia that the entire population of Olivos was here, and it certainly looked that way. It's quite a large place with lots of tables, and it was so packed that we had to wait to get seats. There was a line-up three deep at the counter — no, I'm not exaggerating — and there was a great deal of laughter and chatting as people made their selections.

Not only was the shop packed, but there were people sitting on benches outside on the sidewalk, many with dogs and even small children in tow. The four legged patrons apparently enjoyed the ice cream as much as the rest of us!

Although I've had excellent ice cream in many Buenos Aires shops, this has to be my favourite. If you are anywhere near Olivos you have to try it — preferably after midnight!

Chapter Nineteen

IN CLOSING

More than any of my other books, this one is a passion project. As I said in the opening chapter, I fell in love with Argentina from the first moment of my first visit, and my passion for this wonderful country, particularly its magnetic capital city of Buenos Aires, only deepens every time I go there. I hope to live many more Argentine *aventuras*, which may well find their way into a second volume one of these days.

I hope you enjoyed my stories, and that I've been able to convey even just a fraction of my feelings for Argentina. Even more, I hope I've inspired you to think about visiting yourself. If you do, email me in advance, and if you are in Buenos Aires during my time there, I'd love to get together over a coffee — or a glass of Malbec!

Saludos!

Helen

ABOUT THE AUTHOR

Helen Wilkie was born and grew up in Scotland, moving to Canada for a yearlong adventure in her early twenties. Fate intervened by introducing her to Felix, her much loved husband, and she stayed. After Felix died in 2008, she began to travel on her own, doing several shorter trips closer to home before venturing south to Argentina.

She is a professional keynote speaker, consultant and author in the field of communication in the workplace. She is also a ghostwriter, helping professionals of all kinds write books on their areas of expertise to raise their professional profiles and promote their businesses. In 2016 she dipped her toe in the waters of fiction writing, with her "boomer lit" series of short stories, "On the Road with Merry", which can be found on Amazon and all the other online bookstores.

She went to Argentina for the first time in 2014, and now spends several months of each year in Argentina and its South American neighbours.

Helen's websites:

Books, book coaching and ghostwriting services:
http://www.mhwilkiebooks.com

Speaking services, including her Buenos Aires keynote, "Rare Steaks, Red Wine, Hot Tango":
http://www.mhwcom.com

Blog where she posts sporadically while she is in Argentina:
http://www.heleninargentina.com
Author page on Amazon:
https://www.amazon.com/-/e/B0034PDYDI
Helen welcomes comments or questions about Argentina, this book or her speaking services. Email her at helen@mhwilkiebooks.com
For ongoing, sporadic news of Helen's upcoming books and adventures, join her mailing list at
http://www.mhwilkiebooks.com

RESOURCES

Here is the contact information for some of the people I mention in the book who have businesses that might help you enjoy your Argentine visit.

CECILIA SIERRA THOMPSON

Cecilia Sierra Thompson is a true Porteña and knows Buenos Aires like the back of her hand. She will be happy to tailor her services to suit your needs, from city tours to places of special interest to you. She will also pick you up at the airport and drop you off when you leave.

Cecilia has rooms available for rent to visitors, but check well in advance as they are often booked.

Reach her at sierrathompson@hotmail.com

LOLA BLACK

If tango is at the heart of your visit to Buenos Aires, you must meet Lola Black, otherwise known as Tango Gypsy. She is a personal concierge, specializing in tango tourism, for short term and expat visitors. She can also arrange everything from medical tourism to football tickets, "puertas cerradas" dinners, pilates/ yoga sessions, cultural events, tango milongas/ classes, etc. More information on her Facebook page at

https://www.facebook.com/Gypsytango/?pnref=about.overview

Lola also has a beautiful apartment in Palermo for rent to visitors. These are often people who take advantage of her tango tourism services. Facebook page for this is at

https://www.facebook.com/TangoGypsy/

LINDA CLAIRE PUIG

If you'd like to continue running your online business while you enjoy Buenos Aires, as I do, I strongly recommend Linda Claire Puig's online course, "Traveling with your Business Made Easy". I took this course before my first extended visit to Argentina and it helped me set myself up for success as a "digital nomad". You can find details at

http://www.travelingwithyourbusinessmadeeasy.com/

VENETIA FEATHERSTONE WITTY

Venetia, owner of Featherstone Photography & Film, is an awarding winning photographer who takes stunning photographs during her worldwide travel adventures. You'll be mesmerized by her short documentary film, **Butterflies of the Sea**, which you can find on YouTube at

http://youtu.be/XsSmFMQS2Ek

Her art photos can be seen and purchased at

https://fineartamerica.com/profiles/venetia-featherstone-witty

She is also available for portraits and other commissions, and you can reach her via her Fine Art America link above.

ALEJANDRO PUERTA

If you're dying to experience tango in Buenos Aires but want to take some lessons before venturing out to the *milongas*, you should definitely work with Alejandro Puerta. He will not only teach you the steps and techniques, but help you understand the background and history of tango, and you can't help picking up some of his passion for the dance.

Check out his website at http://alejandropuerta.com and contact him at tango@alejandropuerta.com

You can see a video of one of my lessons with Alejandro at http://www.heleninargentina.com/?p=451

Two useful organizations to help you get to know Buenos Aires:

BUENOS AIRES INTERNATIONAL NEWCOMERS (BAIN)

Members of BAIN are often long-term visitors or expats living in the city, but they also welcome visitors passing through. They are from many countries, and I've met some fascinating people there. Even if you're just in Buenos Aires for a short time, you'll be welcome at BAIN. Check out the website at https://baindowntown.com/

INTERNATIONS

I actually joined InterNations in Toronto, where I've met lovely people from around the world, including Argentina. It's an international organization with branches in most major cities, including Buenos Aires. They have monthly events, usually held in bars or restaurants in Palermo, but I find them a bit too crowded and noisy. However, I do enjoy several of their special interest groups, including those focusing on tango, speaking Spanish and cultural events. Find the Buenos Aires site at

https://www.internations.org/buenos-aires-expats